MORE PRAISE FOR DEAR DEEDEE

The magic and joy of an intimate conversation is hard to renounce. We simply need to share our stories, and Kat Meads does just that in this charming and chatty epistolary memoir to a beloved, pretend niece. Family lore, life wisdom, and real affection abound in these letters. In our current zeitgeist of swift and glib communication, Meads swims upstream past 280 characters of a tweet, texts open to misinterpretation, deadening email chains, to remind us all of the delight in the art of letter writing. *Dear DeeDee* is an absolute pleasure to read.

—Natalie Serber, author of *Shout Her Lovely Name* and *Community Chest*

DEAR DEEDEE

Kat Meads

Regal House Publishing

Published by
Regal House Publishing, LLC
Raleigh, NC 27612
All rights reserved

ISBN -13 (paperback): 9781646030156
ISBN -13 (epub): 9781646030422
Library of Congress Control Number: 2020930419

Interior and cover design by Lafayette & Greene
lafayetteandgreene.com
Cover images © by Flipser and ACS-Images/Shutterstock

Regal House Publishing, LLC
https://regalhousepublishing.com

The following is a work of creative nonfiction created by the author.
Some names, individuals, characters, places, items, brands, events, etc.
were either the product of the author or were used fictitiously. Any
name, place, event, person, brand, or item, current or past, is entirely
coincidental.

Printed in the United States of America

ATTICS. PAPER(S). EVERYONE I LOVED.

West Coast
Monday, Feb. 5

~~Dear,~~
~~Dearest,~~
~~Darling DeeDee,~~
~~Darling niece,~~
~~Greetings,~~

DeeDee,

Can we agree? Beginnings are…challenging. Where to plunge in? How to choose among the millions of possibilities? Since you are and ever have been a more confident sort—unafraid of worms, unfazed by math, un-intimidated by direct and noisy challenges to your opinion—my fainthearted reaction is likely anathema. And although I don't expect you to fully appreciate the advancement in family fortunes your attitude represents, I'd ask you to bear in mind that, for the bulk of your ancestresses, confidence wasn't an outlook easily attained. (Grumpiness, yes; confidence, no.) Literature teaches us to lead with force, provocation, mystery, feeling. "They shoot the white girls first." "We had the car so we went." "He stood at the back gateway of the abattoir, hands thrust into his pockets, stomach rigid with the ache of want." In every case one wants to read what comes next. But will you want to read what I write in these notes to you? Will you feel the least bit interested in what I am inclined to share? I'm aware; I realize. The very fact that I ask signals misgiving when I'm supposed to lead with the surety of force, provocation, mystery, feeling. I will—promises rendered—attempt to do better next time.

Love from over this-away,
Aunt K

West Coast
Wednesday, Feb. 14

DeeDee,

The attic of your grandparents' farmhouse. How well do you remember it? Wasps, canning jars, camping canteens, broken rocking chairs, steamer trunks, heaps of woolen blankets, your grandmother's out-of-fashion "church" hats. Choking heat, March through October. To reach it, one had to scale ladder-steps nailed to the closet wall; then, at the top, cling with one hand while the other knocked aside the plywood hatch. When I was five, part of the attic's attraction was its away away-ness, a quiet spot for me, myself, and I. The other was a pile of discarded schoolbooks under the western eave, among them *Luck and Pluck*, illustrated. Never underestimate the power of association. Never imagine you escape what impresses you as a child.

Love and hugs,
Aunt K

DeeDee,

This will (or should) strike you as odd: my girlfriend duties as a high school senior covered writing my boyfriend's community college term papers. All very fraudulent, all very corrupt, but since my high school English teacher also had me write her husband's community college term papers, my sense of what was and wasn't corrupt had assistance in the skewing. Truth be told, I took the teacher's ghostwriting assignment as a mark of special favor, my study halls devoted to "higher-level" compositions. As was later revealed, whatever I penned on my boyfriend's behalf ("Witch Among Witches: Lady Macbeth," "Odors and Arsenic in 'A Rose for Emily'") amounted to useless effort. My boyfriend's instructor had a crush on him and would have recorded at least a B in his grade book whatever I, via my boyfriend, turned in. Did I care about my useless labor or the crush? In passing.

Love,
Aunt K

DeeDee,

This morning I've been reminiscing about an office supply store in Edenton, a town where, once upon a time, fifty-one rebellious women boycotted English tea. Paper fiends (and I am one) *cannot* pass an office supply store, whatever its state of decline, without a browse. Inside this establishment, heroically holding on despite yet another economic downturn, were more flies than customers. Hives of dust on every shelf. Opening the front door reanimated the dust and flies but never the two proprietors, seated along the back wall in matching chairs. My friend Lynne and I always took our time inspecting the merchandise, settled up in cash, reluctant to leave, certain there'd be no yellowing index cards in that building, on that street, possibly in the entire town, on our next pass-through. And so it happened. You can insure a house or boat from those premises now, but you can't purchase index cards.

Big smooch,
Aunt K

DeeDee,

My first college Christmas, your father—who has always known his sister's heart without obtrusive questioning—gifted me a Random House dictionary that, according to the bathroom scales, weighed in at eleven pounds. In the photo of me hefting it, it's an armful. Other photos of the day feature your lovely mother in suede bellbottoms and fuchsia turtleneck and your dad's never-ending sideburns. Your grandmother thought my skirt too short, my hair too long, but she and your granddad couldn't have been happier that the three of us had come home, driven east, together. Everyone I loved was alive then. In its original meaning, nostalgia meant longing for a place rather than the past. Or so I read recently. And then I stopped reading to wonder: why not both?

Love,
Aunt K

DeeDee,

At your age, I longed deeply to be thirty. Before beginning this note, I tried to nail down why. My rearview-mirror reckoning may not account for *every* factor, but I feel *reasonably* certain that the *primary* reasons I looked forward to spectacular payoffs in my fourth decade were (in no particular order): knowledge accrued, character solidified, energy intact, confidence high, crow's feet charming. In fact, my thirties did start off well. When I needed a job, I found one. When I needed a fuck, I found one of those too. Although I was still (as now) playing catch up on the reading front, I stopped undervaluing my own reader's opinion. Socially and romantically I could still be fooled by bluff and bluster, but it happened less frequently and in most arguments I better held my own. In front of mirrors, I moaned less. The body I had was the body I had. Laudable progress, maturity achieved on multiple fronts. But then, when I was thirty-five and he sixty-seven, your grandfather died and I became a child again, utterly lost and struggling.

Love,
Aunt K

FATALISM. FAITH. A COW.

DeeDee,

Since long-dead ancestors hold little interest for me, why expect otherwise of you? I've been thinking, though: perhaps both of us should make more of an effort in that regard? Concede the ego-bashing fundamental that we didn't spontaneously create ourselves. Acknowledge the line-up of past mortals neither of us saw, heard, or spat up on but without whom we'd not exist. "I always go white as a sheet when bored," Edith Sitwell once quipped. I hope you don't lose color, I hope that's not your reaction, when my notes arrive. But even if it is and you send evidence of your pasty face to drive home the point, I'll probably not cease and desist. Your mother—if you ask, if it's just the two of you in the room at the time—will likely reveal why. Within the family, mine is the dog-with-bone reputation. Once keen on a notion, etc.

Love,
Aunt K

DeeDee,

I've seen at least two battered photographs of my and your dad's paternal great-grandparents (your great-great). Where those photographs are, in whose house or trunk or bureau, I couldn't say. (But I can investigate, if you'd like. Someone in the extended family must know where they hide.) Your great-great grandmother looked as if she could lift an ailing cow to its feet; your great-great grandfather seemed stretched taut by a bitter wind, leaving to posterity a vivid impression of the twin images of farming life: hard labor, grievous setback. As far as has been *expressed* within family lore, your paternal family history presents less turbulent than taxing. Steady labor, erratically rewarded. An occasional "good year" to sweeten the vinegary rest. You are not of an age to binge-watch Dust Bowl documentaries, but in one of the more famous, the narrator characterizes those desperate farmers as "next year" people—as in people who believed their situation would/had to improve the following year. Coastal Carolina farmers whose fields regularly flooded shared the same hope, the same reasoning. Is there a farmer anywhere who doesn't?

Happy almost-spring,
Aunt K

DeeDee,

As mirrors confirm, you have your dad's hooked nose and someone's curly hair but overall resemble your mother. Shared bloodline notwithstanding, you escaped becoming a remake of your paternal great-great grandmother. Since such is the case, I hope you have also been spared *some* degree of body botheration in these slim and exceedingly body-conscious times. The qualifier because what female escapes appearance anxiety altogether? None I know, have known, or read about. Even the beauteous V. Woolf self-reported her "ugliness." If you're supposing the comment that Virginia looked as if she'd "been pulled backwards through a hedge" affirms Virginia's self-criticism, rethink. That Rebecca West remark refers to Virginia's clothes, wardrobe, presentation—not to the frame and flesh on which those disorderly clothes hung. (See what I did there? Tossed in a literary anecdote to postpone admitting what I'd rather not.) Female insecurity in the looks department gives every indication of being a regenerative, evergreen malaise. Even to type those words makes me peevish. However: the deal I struck with myself when I started these notes was not to pretend there'd been progress where there'd been none, or that, gazing back from the advantage of a riper age, I'd describe my own twenties as a period of pure nirvana. Those years were nothing of the sort. I spent most of the decade unhinged and terrified.

Time out,
Aunt K

DeeDee,

I'd have written sooner, but I was waiting for my temper to cool. Since that adjustment took the better part of two days, I'd appreciate it if we kept those recovery stats to ourselves. Your extended family has never gone in for ranting of any sort, outbreaks of which are viewed as unseemly and conspicuously self-indulgent. Extended pique of the sort your aunt just indulged in? A disgrace to one and all. Onward. Before you joined us, our immediate family was a uniformly blue-eyed crew, shades of blue the differential among us. My eyes are darker than your father's, his darker than your grandfather's but quite close to your grandmother's hue. None of us smile with bee stung lips. Your grandmother's skin "never burned" when she sunbathed—a sparing your dad and I coveted, since we shared your grandfather's quick-to-flare paleness accented with freckles. At the beach, regardless, your dad and I stayed all day in the blistering sun. In the late afternoon—and not until—your grandfather joined us. Prior to, he worked on jigsaw puzzles inside the cottage. I could try to describe my six-year-old's squeal, the whirly excitement of seeing him crest the dune, available at last to take me past the breakers. But I wouldn't succeed.

Love,
Aunt K

DeeDee,

Your grandfather was fond of redheads (which is probably the reason your grandmother disliked them), but since no family reunions are currently scheduled, I thought: why not? Next questionable decision: applying the "red mahogany" tint myself. Since the bathroom here is nowhere near spacious, the splatter didn't have far to travel when rainbow-ing the walls. Another problem: I'd assembled too few towels. Another, another problem: I was short a mirror. Covering every strand on the back of one's head is harder than advertised. During the interminable wait for my new color to "set," sequestered in the bathroom with coloration trash, I fell victim to peroxide reveries. After one summer break, all the surfer dudes in my high school showed up with orange hair. Had they made a pact? Thrown a party to douse each other with the burning stuff? So many details I'd ask after now, dumped back into the then. Tomorrow, at the office, I'll be treated to the following reactions (in order): startle, stare, stuttered remarks regarding my "new look." First impression/ expression: that's what I'll be monitoring. Taken by surprise, people generally need a few blinks to bluff.

Love,
Aunt K

DeeDee,

If I ever gave the impression that securing a paycheck under western skies was a snap, let me here correct that falsehood. I interviewed constantly when I first arrived—constantly and increasingly frantically as my set-aside "settle in" funds dwindled. During an interview to teach at a prep school located next to the freeway, I was far, far too upfront in confirming my limited competencies. Voicing my fourth or so "not previously, no," I began to rue the waste of an afternoon (applying makeup, finding the place, lolling in the parking lot for thirty minutes in order to step into the building precisely on time). Eventually I also broke off eye contact. (Why keep up the charade?) Oddly, given those developments, my interviewer remained brightly enthusiastic— and a little too *familiar*—guiding me along the hallway. Back in my rental, I launched into a bout of frenzied cleaning, scrubbing the bathtub in such a way as to throw my back out. When the call came, offering me the job, I had just returned to something like careful mobility. But as if to remind my brain what it shouldn't have forgotten, a muscle in my back spasmed at the news. Economically perilous, turning down that job. The correct choice, nevertheless. The handsy interviewer would have been my direct "superior." Not a happy arrangement.

Love,
Aunt K

DeeDee,

When your grandmother's father, Mr. Bob, came to live out his final years with his married daughter, he brought along his cow. The first time I read "Once upon a time...there was a moocow coming along the road," instead of Joyce's Ireland I pictured our dirt road, Mr. Bob and cow loping along at a leisurely pace, en route to our house. The cow reference suggests Mr. Bob was a farmer as well, but that wasn't the case. Primarily he worked as a carpenter and, on the side, built coffins for the local undertaker. More profitably, he owned a pacer that he raced on Saturdays. The reason I assume you've heard none of this is that Mr. Bob— according to unanimous judgment—doted on your dad, thought nothing finer, etc., and therefore your dad, wary of favorites, would have avoided the Mr. Bob topic in order to avoid admitting he counted as that very thing in Mr. Bob's estimation. (Have I guessed correctly?) I had it "in my head," as your grandmother would say, that it was Mr. Bob who taught your dad, in short pants and sailor middy, to cuss. I've since been corrected, that training provided by two of Mr. Bob's prankster, babysitting sons.

Love,
Aunt K

DeeDee,

You may disagree a little or a lot but you'll not dissuade me. By age five children understand everything there is to understand about power and its exercise from observing their inner circle(s). (I include you in the roundup.) Who has power, who wants it, and what a certain percentage of the crowd are willing to do, have done, and are doing to get it. That sort of understanding. In terms of perception, the innocence of childhood is severely overplayed. I appreciate the cultural impulse to maintain the fiction; nevertheless, the innocence claim itself is false and mildly insulting. Already you're bored by and with this monotonously pontificating note. So now I'll add irritation to the mix by writing this: if boredom counts as the biggest blip of the day, celebrate. A passing annoyance, boredom. Nothing more, nothing less.

Hopping off my soapbox (for now),
Aunt K

DeeDee,

When feelings "ran hot" at a family get-together, one of the less excitable adults typically drew breath and preambled: "I don't think...," while in fact thinking furiously about how best to avoid a full-scale squabble. As a tactic, the dodge worked reasonably well as long as no one elaborated. "I don't think I understand what you're saying" of course meant that the previous statement had not only been thoroughly understood but had given vivid offense. Thereafter, the offender had one chance and one chance only for a do-over. By and large our clan seems to be/have been think-better-of-it practitioners, which is far from saying that every squabble is, was, or could be sidestepped. The family's grudge-holding champ thus far: your paternal great-grandmother. If a grandchild fell in her flowerbed, she held a grudge. If a visitor interrupted her supper, she held a grudge. If her sister Inez took too long making a Scrabble move, she held a grudge. Did your great-grandmother exist, moment to moment, spoiling for a fight? Let's just say she tapped into a reservoir of resentments with *exceptional* speed. No shortage of reasons for any 1890-born female to resent the fortresses of power and a woman's backstairs pantry space within. But your great-grandmother's active expectation of disrespect frequently guaranteed that the assumption bore fruit. Rock and hard place.

Love,
Aunt K

DeeDee,

The phrase may have worn itself out by the time you came along, but, put to a vote, I'm pretty sure your dad and I would agree that during our brat years your grandmother's go-to counter was: *Can't help that.* "Go to sleep."/ "Not tired."/"Can't help that." "Do your homework."/ "Too hard."/ "Can't help that." "Go visit your aunt."/ "She smells funny."/ "Can't help that." Advantages on her side? Autopilot resistance to our resistance, no additional time or energy wasted on tailored-to-the-occasion comebacks. Was your grandmother parroting her own mother's solution to shutting up children or did the phrase, newly minted, first pop out during a standoff with your dad and me? And what did your grandmother, self-to-self, take that expression to mean? That she personally lacked the power to alter the situation or that, in a fait accompli universe, no human agent wielded such power? Questions unasked.

Love,
Aunt K

DeeDee,

You've heard the story of the cousin who'd "carry a boulder for you for twenty years" if you asked nicely, but if you *told* him to do it… Recalcitrance. Pretty standard Southern hiccup. As a teenager, digging in my heels over nothing earth-shatteringly important, I was advised by someone I didn't otherwise despise to "just mouth agreement" and save myself "gobs of bother." Digging in one's heels, affably appearing to agree. Both regional staples. What I reiterate here, you no doubt figured out rolling around in your crib. A Southern "uh-huh" doesn't necessarily (or even frequently) indicate accord. Uttered one Southerner to another, its equivocal nature is taken for granted and otherwise known as oiling the wheels of polite discourse. Why this harping? To prevent you from being too terribly thrown by the deficit of surface courtesies once you venture beyond the Southern wild. You'll be thrown to some extent, regardless. There's no remedying that.

Love,
Aunt K

West Coast
Wednesday, March 13

DeeDee,

In future, should you run short of dog names, consider browsing
the branches of your dad's family tree: Moody, Benoni, Butler,
Carrie, Attie, Althea. The higher branches are thick with preachers
and their persevering wives, true, and that aspect alone might
put you off the repurposing. But later begets passed on both
the pulpit and showboat pieties. One of your great-uncles, as a
child, *did* attempt to baptize his cat in molasses but was feverish
with chicken pox at the time; no eyewitness credited a fervency
of faith. For several years your grandfather managed to put off
becoming a deacon by telling the church committee he "liked
to dance"—an admission that also implied he wasn't opposed
to taking a nip of whiskey behind the community hall when
not cuttin' the rug with his wife. He lost that standoff, twice
serving as deacon. When asked to run for honorary mayor of the
community, he took a more active role in the dissuading, going
house to house, asking that no one vote for him. Since no one
voted for the other nominees either, the honorary mayor notion
died on the vine. To belabor the obvious: being comfortable
in his own skin made your grandfather something of a rarity,
inside the family and out. And although he, himself, didn't expect
everyone to be like everyone else, he understood that "fitting in"
counted as a top priority for most of the people he knew, and
that was fine by him too.

Love,
Aunt K

West Coast
Thursday, March 14

DeeDee,

Not one of ours (in terms of blood kin), Preacher Getts presided over the pulpit of Providence Baptist during the years your dad and I still counted as churchgoers. Radically overworked, Preacher Getts. In addition to carrying the weight of lost souls (in the abstract), in the flesh he was obligated to visit the community's bereaved and stricken, entice flagrant backsliders back into the fold, and offer counsel to the theologically confused. While your grandmother hung back on the porch, Preacher Getts shared the backyard bench with me, called in to discuss the usual kid probe: who made God? Apparently I had no difficulty with world creation in six days but the conundrum of how the starter got started crinkled my brain. For the guidance session, I wore red shorts and a striped top; Preacher Getts wore his non-Sunday khaki. A lanky creature, sandy-haired, infinitely patient, not in the least condescending to his child audience, Harlan Getts appeared visibly troubled by my spiritual disquiet, my doubt adding to his burden. After thirty minutes or so, we were both weary. "We'll talk again," he said, but I don't recall that we did, just we two. Surely I'd remember, if so?

Love,
Aunt K

P.S. "Religion...the great anonymous writer of threatening letters." —Dorothy Baker. (Read her.)

DeeDee,

Don't tell your dad, but I just returned from a California-style "retreat." (Incentives: an officemate dared me to come with, then sealed the deal with a week of lunch bribes.) Directly after work on Friday, we saddled up and travelled three hours to a mountainside enclave of kerosene-lit cabins. (Don't tell your grandmother, either. She'd be appalled by such light-source backsliding in her child.) Technically, we weren't supposed to bring any entertainment beyond ourselves, but I sneaked in one of those itty bitty book lights that eat up batteries and a copy of *Neuromancer*. My officemate was more put off by the "organic" toilet than I, but the staff's heads-up that baby rattlesnakes had been spotted outside our cabin door the week before succeeded in freaking us both. What couldn't be bitched about: the valley light show, courtesy of our darker quarters. Despite the viper threat, by hour fifteen or so your flatlander aunt *had* begun to veg a little, perched on a slope—the point of the exercise, after all. Then came the knock. A gaggle of Jehovah's Witnesses had managed to circumvent two locked gates and poisonous wildlife to make their pitch. Par for the course, your dad would say, so (again, please) kindly refrain from supplying him the ammunition.

Love,
Aunt K

DeeDee,

The afternoon our Sunbeam leader, Mrs. Roberts, turned into the driveway of a house on the swampy side of the causeway, it felt weird. Weird because no traveller reached E. City via Route 34 without passing the house, and from the recesses of Mrs. Roberts's backseat I suddenly realized I'd never asked—or wondered—who lived there during any previous pass-by. Inside, we trailed Mrs. Roberts through a chilly hallway into a dim living room, floorboards covered by a linoleum rug worn through in spots, its florals rubbed pale. Our hosts sat close to the oil furnace that shot out into the room, and because the room held little else besides their chairs, we Sunbeams had plenty of space to fan out and perform "large." Our usual repertoire spanned the (obligatory) "Jesus Wants Me for a Sunbeam," "Jesus Loves Me," and a group rendition of the 23rd Psalm, two of those three (or three of the three?) cringingly self-centered, given our mission. I can't remember whether the two women were sisters or cousins or just friends sharing a home to pool scant resources. But their unwavering smiles were very similar as was their palpable desire to prove themselves a grateful, responsive audience. I suppose it was the combination of physical frailty and heroic effort that stuck with me. That, and how awful and awkward it felt to finish up and leave that sad place without, as Sunbeams, having done much to brighten it.

Love,
Aunt K

DeeDee,

Another road trip! And happily do I report this one featured neither vipers nor viper threat. However: if precipitous drop-offs unnerve you, steer clear of Henry Miller's post-Paris neighborhood, a mind-boggling mix of rock and wave and cliff. My reason for crashing the scene: co-snooping. Invited to teach a summer workshop, my friend wanted to check out the facilities before signing on the dotted line. A staff member met us in the parking lot. (To get inside the inner sanctum as a visitor, escort required.) Nothing short of spectacular, the compound's oceanfront views, but when the eye turned from natural wonders to the complex itself...time warp. Here the '60s came, settled, and refused to budge. No locks on any doors (bathrooms included), dining communal, clothing optional (but scorned) when taking a dip in the hot springs. The seminar rooms contained floor pillows but no chairs because "people prefer to lounge," our handler said, managing to imply that sitting upright on furniture was both regressive and aggressive. Instructors, we learned, were assigned bedrooms next to their seminar rooms in order to facilitate "availability" at any hour of the twenty-four anyone elected to avail. This was the point of informational exchange at which I'd have bolted, but my friend stuck it out, though less sunnily. (I'd wager we were pegged for standoffish privacy mongers right off the bat.) As with other free-and-easy enclaves, there were plenty of rules—they just weren't posted. Attempting to go with the flow, we offered hearty hellos to the first person who crossed our path, only to be chided for "breaking the silence" and "interrupting his meditation." But we didn't know! We didn't know!

Love,
Aunt K

DeeDee,

And how are you spending your undergrad Sundays? Cramming for Monday midterms? Throwing back tequila shots? Skateboarding? Since your seventh days have always been yours to arrange, envisioning your dad in a Sunday School classroom, followed by a sanctuary regroup for the everyone/all-in sermon, must be a mental stretch. Nonetheless, every Sunday morning there he'd be—in church with his chums and me with mine. Inviolate tradition: before Preacher Getts launched into his own supplications, he called upon devout octogenarian Hal Cox to deliver the morning prayer. Voice quavering, breath a wheezy whistle, Brother Cox gripped the pew ahead to physically sustain himself during that lengthy appeal. (His moral muscle needed no such reinforcement.) Long after your dad and I spent our Sundays churchless, we used "Hal the Prayer Cox" as shorthand to describe any particularly numbing interlude. Although your dad and his Brylcreem-ed gang got to pass around the collection plates on special occasions, no female ever touched those wooden bowls. Manly work, it was supposed.

Love,
Aunt K

DeeDee,

Two of your paternal great-uncles (neither the cat baptizer) served overseas in the Second World War, one as an infantryman, the other as an air traffic controller. Multiple copies of their official, in-uniform, sepia-tinted headshots were mailed home and distributed among close relatives. Without exception those portraits were framed and prominently displayed, as if the fixities of pose and arrangement would counteract the volatilities of war. Your great-uncles were both fortunate; they survived. But once home, neither spoke of his military service or the war, those experiences sealed up and locked away. While his brothers were doing their patriotic duty, your grandfather, doing his, stayed home to farm. Your grandfather and great-grandfather planted mostly cotton. As a kid, your dad gazed upon cotton fields. I never did but convinced myself that a cotton crop must look like a bunch of bird nests—if bird nests were snowy white and planted in rows. What I actually saw from the breakfast table were cornfields, morning glories curling around the stalks nearest the path, and every now and again a rabbit, also breakfasting.

Love,
Aunt K

DeeDee,

And now I'm feeling abashed at having failed to mention your grandmother's contribution to the war effort. An inadvertent slight—leaving out the women—but still inexcusable. As in other coastal counties, the married females of your grandmother's community served as "watchers," scanning the night skies for enemy planes. One night of every fourteen your grandmother occupied a government hut that had been erected between the grain bins and railroad tracks and outfitted with peepholes and a telephone. If either she or her partner spotted suspicious aircraft, the spotter was to call in and report immediately. When I asked your grandmother (I *did* quiz her on this issue) whether or not she'd found staying awake all night after a hard day's work difficult, she answered (rather sharply): "Not in the least." Coffee, gossip, and sewing projects filled up the time counter-spying left idle. When I asked to be shown the exact coordinates of her surveillance, she at first refused ("There's nothing there!") but gave in because I pestered. We visited the spot in glary daylight, the sky pale blue, not inky. Through a squint, I could barely ID the raven flying past.

Awake this night,
Aunt K

DeeDee,

Other grandma info you may be missing: as a newlywed, she worked the fields alongside your grandfather and great-grandfather. Pregnant with your dad, she still helped handpick the year's cotton crop, a canvas sack slung across her belly. Later, she drove the flatbed truck, the clutch of which defied her. Her jerky shifting on one outing pitched your grandfather, wrestling seed bags, off the truck. Eventually she noticed—but not right away. Your grandfather (so goes the story) didn't complain about the dumping but teased her mercilessly about the drive-on. Your dad adored piloting the flatbed truck (or any truck) as well as the tractor but despised, as anyone would, shoveling drains. I never shoveled drains but, lured by the almighty dollar, hoed weeds—or did until encountering any sort of snake, poisonous or non-, after which I "knocked off." Your grandfather kept his account books in the attic. In one entry, he lists his children's wages for the day: $12.25 to your (more persevering) dad; $1.25 to your aunt who, though she failed to finish hoeing a single row, was paid for an hour of sitting in the clearing with the dogs, singing to herself.

Love,
Aunt K

DeeDee,

We chatted last night, your grandmother and I. She was having trouble sleeping and because of the three-hour time difference assumed I'd still be awake and her call "wouldn't disturb me." She wouldn't have disturbed me if she'd called at five a.m., her time, instead of two—but that I didn't tell her. Your grandmother wanted to know whether or not I felt I'd had a "happy childhood." Happy childhoods loom large in your grandmother's consciousness because hers wasn't. How could it have been? Her own mother took to bed in her fifties, depressed and exhausted, and died when your grandmother was eleven— not the sort of emotional vacancy that ever gets filled, though your grandmother tried to fill it with us, her children, keeping your dad and me close, doing/overdoing for us, catering to our whines and whims, attending every ballgame, entertaining our friends, permitting us the run of the house for whatever we wanted the run of it for, cooking for packs of kids on short notice, welcoming anyone we wanted to hang with, filling in, on demand, in backyard games of badminton or indoor games of gin rummy. "Always hovering," as she described it, wanting me to contradict that harsh assessment, reassure her that I'd wanted her as involved in my life as she'd been. Growing up, I probably did wish she'd been a little less on hand, a little less in my business. I had the luxury of such complaints.

Love,
Aunt K

DeeDee,

Have you pegged your aunt an ardent sentimentalist, overly attached to childhood panoramas and visions? Admittedly, in these notes there's not much of the outer world—bombings or clonings or princesses losing their HRH titles. All very insular, all very *place* oriented, these communiqués. "The whole concept of place is dead and it's nostalgia to cling to it," William Burroughs once squawked (and not in the throes of a heroin high). And yet, and yet: that son of the Midwest returned to the Midwest, age sixty-seven, and didn't again leave. I used to think constantly moving house prevented early-onset nostalgia. (A dippy notion. No one else's life and origins are more interesting than one's own.) My new working theory pimps nostalgia as connection, a connection with who I was and therefore am. Unfortunately that face-saving spin ignores a basic horror. The past is set. No revising or improving *it*.

Enough,
Aunt K

SCREEN DOORS. SILLINESS. SOUTHERN HOSTESS DISEASE.

DeeDee,

My sense is that you operated as a craftier child, adolescent, and teen than either your dad or I, viewing adults as specimens that, though (of necessity) had to be tolerated, were not entirely to be trusted. (Have I come close?) In any event, little could be pried out of you that you chose not to reveal which, on various celebratory occasions, made it harder than strictly necessary to select your gift. A fairly forthcoming child, the older I got the more I lied because I'd conveniently learned how and lying helped circumvent what proved to be an aggravating personal defect. Although I seldom *volunteered* information, as soon as friend or stranger asked, on and on I'd chatter, disclosing more than intended, obedient to the Southerner's code of cordiality, ensuring the questioner's ease at the expense of my own. Southern hostess disease, I used to call that abominable reflex until a comment by Sir Kingsley Amis suggested I'd gone too narrow in my labeling. "I always tend to fill in conversational gaps, merely to avoid general awkwardness, a trait that has brought me from close-mouthed buggers cheeky accusations of being a chatterbox." Who, I ask, would have taken Sir Kingsley for a chatterer?

Love,
Aunt K

West Coast
Wednesday, April 3

DeeDee,

Do you know the novel *A Charmed Life?* Allegedly one of Mary
McCarthy's "less contemptuous" works. I sought it out for its
under-disguised Cape Cod setting. If you decide to pick up a
copy, skip the play-reading chapter. It will only turn you off
1950s novels altogether. I mention the book because McCarthy
has main character Martha declare: "In the country...you had
to be *disponible*. Otherwise, people would say you were a snob."
Your country grandmother would indeed have been mortified
if anyone considered her a "snob," a term she defined (in the
practical sense) as the failure to mingle with gusto. So: to qualify
as a non-snob (from your grandmother's perspective), one had
to be forever welcoming of interruption and interrupters.

Feeling exhausted by proxy,
Aunt K

DeeDee,

Just last week, an administrator sharing my going-down elevator
decided he'd also share—supposedly in jest—how I "came
across to people." The verdict: "something between intimidating
and folksy." It was the end of a workday. Either because I was
tired or irritated or irritated and tired, I snarled: "One or the
other: intimidating or folksy. Can't be both." (Since he's not one
of the someones who can fire me, why not trade insolence for
insolence?) Bad manners aside, I relate this incident to encourage
you—as soon as can be managed—to give up the dream of
controlling what anyone thinks (or says) about you. It's a fool's
errand. If you consult your grandmother, she'll disagree because
1) she's put countless hours into the task and 2) thus far she
hasn't been cornered in an elevator and disabused of what she
takes to be her success. Since chances are slim you'll chose to
live in a community as (publicly) polite as your grandmother's,
I'm trying to save you both time and grief. It's never too early
for a female to assume a love-me-or-get-out-of-my-face stance.
Until the age of twenty-seven, your aunt (fruitlessly) worked to
appear less eccentric than she incorrigibly is. At twenty-eight,
she belatedly recalibrated. A fancy way of saying I came round
to: *fuck that shit.*

Love,
Aunt K

West Coast
Monday, April 8

DeeDee,

Speaking of: if you've got to stomp through mud and muck, why not stomp in utilitarian black boots? And yet when the Brontë sisters stomped into the Haworth stationery to load up on writing supplies, their unladylike footwear offended the proprietor. My bet: Emily B. didn't give shitsticks what the town's stationer or any other citizen thought, but Charlotte would have been stung by such criticism. An advantage to being sister-less? Neither you nor I got sent into "society" dressed as one of a matching pair. And yet duplication dilemmas *will* crop up. When Sharon S. and I fixated on the same two-piece bathing suit at the Galleon in Nags Head, we had to negotiate (strenuously) who bought the blue version and who the green. We'd go as far as appearing in the same style, but the very same suit? Ixnay to that. Similarly, during a wet June on Martha's Vineyard, a sister chambermaid and I fancied the identical yellow rain slicker. I left the shop wearing neon green—a sacrifice in the name of friendship but also a good call in other respects. During that and successive rainy seasons, my green slicker and I proved inseparable. Wore that thing till it lost all capacity to repulse water.

Still dry in California,
Aunt K

DeeDee,

Do females make and discard friends with greater ease and swiftness than their male counterparts? (Possibly.) Are we *that* confident of our charming ways and boundless capacity for instant intimacy? (Rash conceit.) Do we imagine there's a limitless supply of gal buddies out there? (That one I can conclusively answer: there's not.) The blunt fact of the matter: being "dropped" by a girlfriend always caused your aunt more heartache than any boyfriend loss. And then there was the domino effect: the next friendship entered into with greater caution, me a less candid/more tentative companion, the new connection compromised from the start, a cool-down anticipated before the relationship had fully warmed. Past and present, would I prefer to proceed less warily? Most definitely I would. But that outlook seems to demand more optimism than our bloodline supplies.

Love,
Aunt K

DeeDee,

Early on, poison ivy was your dad's implacable nemesis. We'd go crashing through the same patch of it at the edge of the swamp or ditch bank and I'd come out utterly unscathed, your father head-to-toe infected. (As is typical, he got the last laugh. He grew out of his allergies; I grew in. Just gazing at poison oak, I break out in hives.) For a week your dad would live pink-spotted in calamine lotion, in bed during the worst of the siege, eyelids swollen nearly shut. Seeing him in that state upset me profoundly. The puffy disfigurement, the smeary pink, his misery and incapacitation. As the younger sister—or just as a kid?—alterations to the status quo jangled. To prevent his scratching what itched, deepening sores and spreading the inflammation, your grandmother stayed at his bedside, held his hand, distracted him. Throughout our childhoods, when either of us was "laid up, feeling puny," your grandfather interrupted his chores to check on us, tiptoeing into the house so as not to disturb if we were snoozing, careful not to let the screen door slam. And yet I always heard his footsteps, no matter how circumspect the approach—listened for it, actually, his concern almost worth getting sick for.

Hoping *you're* not feeling puny,
Aunt K

DeeDee,

Prevalence of screen doors/incidents of screen doors slammed in Southern Lit. Doesn't this strike you as a "Jeopardy" category in the making? "I don't know what the South ought to be," Harry Crews mused about his homeland, "only what it has become. Corrupted all the way to quaint." Do screen doors now classify as "quaint," do you suppose? And why did my last night's mind spin catch and hold on the subject? I do remember a classmate objecting to the "screen door assumption," which he interpreted as ignorance (given the number of air-conditioned households below the Mason-Dixon) and a prime example of regional slur. When your grandparents bought their first window air conditioner, I was *delighted*. A cool(er) house on a sweltering day! Come the evening, we still flung open windows and solid doors to the shrieks and whumps of the swamp, a practice I found equally satisfying. I can't think it preferable: falling asleep to a mechanized hum, shut off from evidence that not *every* creature within hollering distance beds down at the very same hour. Your baby brain (also) got lullabyed by swamp tunes—your dad made certain of that.

Love,
Aunt K

DeeDee,

Whether or not you noticed, from the time you were a tot, greeting you was, for me, an exercise in conflict. Much as I wanted to grab and "hug on you" a little or a lot, I'd noticed you were a squirmer in such situations. I, too, had been a squirmer. Your father, on the other hand, stoically and stiffly endured affectionate seizure by the relatives, wearing a look of pained grievance. Although expressions of grievance were acceptable in a boy child, in a girl child (squirmy or no) frowns were decidedly frowned upon. In the privacy of her home, your grandmother was a reasonably tolerant parent, but in the public domain her notion of what passed muster erred on the side of strict. I once made the mistake of frownily complaining to the coffee shop waitress about fingerprints in my Wonder Bread sandwich. Bratty behavior to be sure, but—in my defense—I gagged easily. When the waitress offered to bring another sandwich, your grandmother declined before I could accept, finished her own chicken salad, paid for both meals (eaten and un-), ushered me out the door and only after we were beyond coffee shop range gave my elbow a very sharp pinch. Needless to say, that trip to town didn't end with coconut squares from the candy counter at Grants.

Off to get a sweet,
Aunt K

West Coast,
Tuesday, April 16

DeeDee,

On the town trip that ended minus a sugar high, my bangs needed trimming—or so your grandmother maintained. Ditches of tears were shed during and after the cutting of your aunt's bangs, upkeep performed by your grandmother and her sewing scissors. Since the goal was a perfectly straight line of hair across my forehead, the quest to make it so led to multiple attempts, each with fewer strands to work with. Your curls, I suspect, prevented experiments in the bangs department as long as your mom was in charge of your coiffure. If tempted to chop some now, have a friend talk you down. (I've already warned against do-it-yourself dye jobs, haven't I?) Your dad's worst haircut was a flattop. Hideous. But since his friends shared the same barber, he was spared the peer ridicule that would have added insult to injury. Your mother's mom, when we met, wore her hair in a chic bob, which, in its uncolored defiance, must have caused quite a stir at the club when first previewed. She had impeccable style, your other grandmother, and unflappable poise. No clubhouse snigger would have thrown her off stride. Is your mother allowing her own hair to gray? If you have a recent photo of the two of you, send a copy west?

Missing you this night,
Aunt K

DeeDee,

As a member of the high school band, your dad—by rights—got to march in E. City's Thanksgiving parade, blowing his trombone and strutting his stuff in a white gabardine uniform with gold epaulets. To "my" Thanksgiving parade, he came garbed in darker attire and waited with your grandparents on Main Street to watch his sixteen-year-old sis roll by in a Chevy convertible stuffed with DAR Good Citizens. (As the only female willing to give up P.E. to declaim on "The Flag—What It Means to Me," my nomination was a lock.) To the girl, our carload wore tweed suits and leather gloves and pillbox hats that happily stayed put at a cruising speed of five miles per hour. From their sidewalk post, your grandparents and dad smiled upon all but waved only to me. A strange sensation, our mutual waving. The parade carrying me forward, away from them, that sudden gulf between us. A similar feeling when your grandparents and I waved goodbye to your dad on the lawn of his college dorm—but worse. We had to wait months to see him again. Freshmen weren't allowed to return home until Thanksgiving.

Love,
Aunt K

DeeDee,

Did you ever see your grandmother's swagger coat? Thirties' vintage, flattering lines, mothballed in the attic. Far too warm for Southern winters, but perfect for my winter in New York. Your mother also offered to lend her faux-fur jacket, but even the faux version looked a little too upscale for where I'd be living/ could afford to live, so I declined to pack it. I *did* make use of your mother's closet the week before my final prom, rummaging through her batch of party and bridesmaid gowns. The dress I settled on—ivory satin, square neckline, tapestry accents— was quite stunning and totally unlike my previous prom duds, which tended toward frill and floaty. Although your prom boycotts hardly raised an eyebrow, in my era the extended family still celebrated dress-up night, stopping by before the "boy" showed up to ooh and ah and snap photos. Reporting it now, the communal look-see seems more touching than irksome. At the time, though, I was "beside myself," fretting that my date would arrive before they left and we'd be subjected to lame jokes and silliness. Familial outbreaks of silliness. Let me think more on this.

Love,
Aunt K

DeeDee,

Here's what's happening here: bookshelves raided for a half-remembered description of female silliness, that search extended because I got distracted by other descriptions, paragraphs, and plots. I'd have saved myself considerable effort if I'd gone straight to the Mitford shelf, which is where I eventually found what I was looking for in *Highland Fling*. Jane Dacre, though "a very ordinary sort of girl,"…"thought by some to be exceptionally stupid," possessed "the sort of feminine astuteness that prevented her from saying silly things." What probably made the description adhere on first reading: real-life acquaintance with Aunt Madeline, an indiscriminate giggler deemed silly by the collective. Before writing to you tonight, I vowed to (also) come up with the name of a silly *male* family member and have: the seldom seen Uncle Milton. Absolutely true (at least in company), Aunt Madeline did divine when enough giggling was enough and cut it short. On the rare occasions we observed Uncle Milton in action, the same could not be said of him.

Love,
Aunt K

DeeDee,

Humor is such a strange beast. What one finds hilarious, another judges sophomoric, etc. As you've serially witnessed, your dad and I are suckers for pratfalls, choreographed or happenstance. Not very sporting of us in the second case, but there it is; it's how we're wired. Whenever *A Shot in the Dark* returned to a theatre anywhere within driving range—noon or midnight showing—we'd be there, front and center, howling at the antics of Inspector Clouseau as if we hadn't previously memorized every speech and tumble. *All of Me* credits still scrolling onscreen, I bolted from my seat to call and prep your dad for Steve Martin dragging himself door to curb and back again, physical comedy at its finest. Watching that scene, I laughed so hard I choked on my own saliva. I did! He (your dad) has said—on record and unequivocally—that he couldn't live with a woman who lacked a sense of humor. But—hasn't it also been your experience?— even minus the shared address, humor helps. Morning-afters are so much less awkward when both parties are inclined to laugh. Both. That's key.

Love,
Aunt K

DeeDee,

Who makes your list of funny authors? I'll not hazard a guess. But I *have* stuck a post-it on the doorknob as reminder to send you the complete works (to date) of the incomparable Nancy Lemann. Read *every* one, but begin where she began, *Lives of the Saints*. ("Oh, I forgot to tell about Percy Chumbley. Percy Chumbley was one of my suitors. Percy Chumbley was the most revolting thing known to man. That's all I have to say about him.") "You either get Lemann or you don't," I was told by a critic who didn't. (He also didn't hail from the South.) When I found a signed copy of Lemann's first novel in her hometown, I walked out of the Garden District Book Shop, nose in the book and promptly fell down three granite steps. And there you have it: humorous symmetry in your aunt's universe. But if *Lives* were only hilarious, I wouldn't be using up aunt chips insisting you read it. Some months after publication, a heartless someone auctioned off Lemann's second book, along with the personal, handwritten note folded inside. *It might not break your heart like the other one—I mean it didn't do as well. But I did put my heart in as much. I mean it broke my heart as much.* Given such evidence of heart and heartlessness, I wouldn't recommend becoming an author.

Love,
Aunt K

DeeDee,

Once upon a time your aunt occupied the same island as Lillian Hellman. Asked how to address a fan note, the local postmistress advised: "Lillian Hellman, Vineyard Haven—that'll get to her." And it did. Ms. Hellman cordially replied. (Inadequately addressed mail delivered! Famous authors responding to reader-strangers! Bygone niceties of a bygone ethos.) Because she'd lived so long "up North," critics seemed to forget Lillian's boil-time in a culture that considered a story told well as good as—if not better than—truth. Those late-in-the-going memoirs served her well, then not so well, but who can deny the dramatic chops of her fictional nonfictions? Who? My second home that winter was the Chilmark library whose shelves gratifyingly stocked everything I ferreted for. The non-insulated cottage I rented on the island's west end had a woodstove and a view of sand dunes (but not waves). For company I had a dewclaw-deformed tabby, as happy as I to take shelter from the ferocious wind. On my days off, on the ratty sofa, I'd read, she'd purr and when the mood struck us we'd shift to gazing at what the wind whipped about outside. Lillian told an interviewer she'd stopped walking the Vineyard beaches because people routinely waylaid her to ask what she was working on. "Never ask a writer what she's working on." Remember that no-no if, on some future seaside stroll, you encounter a famous scribe.

Love,
Aunt K

West Coast
Sunday, April 28

DeeDee,

Last night I watched a documentary about Lewis Carroll, aka Reverend Charles Dodgson, Church of England deacon, math whiz, inventor, photographer, migraine sufferer, life-long stammerer and famous/infamous friend of real-life Alice Liddell, the inspirational force behind *Alice in Wonderland*. In addition to assorted weigh-ins on whether or not Carroll was an active or "repressed" pedophile or neither, the documentary offered up this fascinating factoid: fitful sleeper Carroll invented something he called a nyctograph to take notes in the dark, loath to abandon bed and light a candle. During that reveal, my jaw went slack with envy. (You, on the other hand, are likely experiencing a surge of gratitude that your insomniac aunt owns no such gizmo.) In the way of such things, treated to visuals of English fields and rabbit paths, I began musing on homegrown fields, this one here, that one there and finally the field between Uncle Herman and Aunt Rosa's house and the Harringtons' house. Even in a community of seen-better-days constructions, the Harringtons' house stood out in its levels of disrepair, a house in which, during my childhood, lived a stammering boy who, you guessed it, turned out to be a math whiz, escaping home and county not through a hedge or a well but by means of a full college scholarship. The world is not as large as it is small, eh?

Love,
Aunt K

West Coast
Monday, April 29

DeeDee,

Just now I'm typing on the keyboard of a Mac Classic II, a dandy machine I've grown attached to—though I do miss twisting a platen knob. From home to here, across nine state lines, I trucked a Brother word processor. Before that upgrade, I had a Brother electronic typewriter and before that a Smith Corona electric typewriter and before *that* your dad's passed down (across?) Olivetti, a manual typewriter whose keys had to be struck with something like fury to leave their mark. Sylvia Plath bought herself the same model Olivetti a month after marrying Ted—surely one of her more sanguine acts. For one of my grade school b-days, your grandparents bought me a "toy" typewriter that, toy-ness aside, competently handled my off-the-cuff correspondence with important, imaginary people. It's one of the relics I *wish* your grandparents' attic still sheltered, but wherever my first typewriter got to, it isn't there. Writing to you, I'd originally planned to go totally retro: fountain pen, swooningly thick, cream-colored stationery. The kink in that plan:

It would have looked something like this ————

Ghastly, agreed? Since I can barely decipher my own handwriting, you—it stands to reason—would have a far worse go of it. And since adding to the difficulty reduces the chances of your reading these notes at all, here I sit, tap, tap, tapping keyboard keys.

Love,
Aunt K

DeeDee,

I mentioned *Alice*'s author. Turns out he also penned a letter writing how-to, *Eight or Nine Wise Words about Letter Writing*. I'm pleased and a smidgen proud that in our correspondence I haven't (as yet) committed **every** faux pas on Carroll's list. For instance, thus far I haven't filled "more than a page and a half with apologies for not having written sooner" or used a postscript to "contain the real gist of the letter." Regarding these imperatives: "don't repeat yourself"; "don't try to have the last word"; "make jesting obvious" to avoid said jest being "taken as earnest" and calling down "very serious consequences"—I fear I stand on shakier ground

Hugs,
Aunt K

DOGS. CARS. VIPERS REDUX.

DeeDee,

Your dad had just turned sixteen the summer he nabbed the coveted job of driving the county's mosquito truck. The familial benefit of that prized contract (or so we thought at the time): our house got triple-fogged with DDT twice a month. Like your dad, I learned to drive a tractor first, truck second, car third. In the latter two categories, I was considered "heavy footed." I liked to see how fast I could take the curves. When I was thirteen and he sixteen, a boy named Earl let me drive his parents' car up and down our dirt road, which I did with enthusiasm, your grandmother watching to make sure I made the driveway turn during each circuit but otherwise letting me have at it. ("If the boy's dumb enough to let her drive…") High on my priority list: make Earl and all the boys on the backseat slide about and squeal. (Did that happen? I choose to remember: yes.) When I was fifteen, new state regulations required that every fifteen-year-old pass a Driver's Training course prior to applying for a license. The basketball coach who also taught Driver's Training offered tips on exactly when and where to accelerate in a curve if fleeing the car behind—or just for the zoom. I passed the road test, no problem, but flunked the eye exam. Where'd it originate, your father's and my myopia? Neither of your grandparents needed specs.

Love,
Aunt K

DeeDee,

In his pre-driving years, your dad's mode of transport was his bike and for summer ballgames he got himself the couple of miles or so from our house to the community's ball diamond by pedaling. Your grandmother and I followed in the Ford Crestliner, arriving in time for the game, if not the warm-up. Usually your dad pitched. Nine innings of pitching tired him out (or so he pretended); homeward bound, he preferred not to pedal. By holding onto the car's door handle, he and his bike zipped along at car speed. I know! Awfully dangerous! He could have been maimed, killed!—but wasn't. Your grandmother drove *very* slowly home, she and your dad discussing the game's highlights through the open window. Me? I was still short enough to stand on the seat between them, nibbling a popsicle and dripping juice. I know! Awfully dangerous! A sudden stop could have sent me flying through the windshield!—but didn't. Whenever she braked, your grandmother flung her arm across my middle to keep me from toppling. I know! Any topple on my part could have broken her arm!—but didn't.

Love,
Aunt K

DeeDee,

For a single year of overlap, your dad's high school bus and my grammar school bus met up twice a day to swap passengers at the corner store in Sligo. Come the afternoon exchange, the bus drivers and the rest of us, ages six to seventeen, needed a fortifying snack. I and my sweet tooth made a dash for the Tootsie Roll aisle. Your dad preferred the sweet and salty combo of Dr. Pepper fizzed with peanuts. Although occasionally he shared a swig of the concoction, I never became a full-fledged convert, put off less by the taste than the bother of all that prep. To get at the gratifications of a Tootsie Roll, you just had to rip open a wrapper. Fun fact: California offers safe haven to a surprising number of Dr. Pepper addicts. I've long lost count of the diet and full strength DPs I've spied on the desks of receptionists as well as veeps, fueling their 9 to 5s. Mention that during my westward ho I toured the famous bottling plant in Dublin, Texas, and—business at hand be damned—I'm pressed for a blow-by-blow account. (Of the DP plant, not my cross-country migration.)

Love,
Aunt K

DeeDee,

Did your dad and I grow up in a "car culture"? I suppose. There was a time when both of us could rattle off the currently driven as well as the previously owned auto in each household of the extended family as well as the community entire, that roll call as easy as naming our dogs. To rachet up the challenge, we'd sometimes match car with dog(s), as in which pets were around when this or that vehicle served as the main ride. Your grandparents' '51 Ford Crestliner: Towser and Tiny. '60 Ford Falcon: Arrowhead and Lady. I could go on, but without substantiation of one or another sort those pair-up claims come off less convincing. For the record: we didn't name cars. Oh, I think I heard a cousin once refer to his junker as "the old jalopy," but that's hardly the equivalent of a "Sue" or a "Travis." Naming a car struck us as precious, the kind of thing families lacking in children and pets would do.

Love and kisses,
Aunt K

DeeDee,

For date nights in high school, your dad borrowed Uncle Herman's newer model Ford. In exchange for the lend-out, once a week Uncle Herman got his car vacuumed, washed and buffed—an arrangement that suited both parties. Your dad's fourth-hand Morris Minor—turquoise, two-door, four cylinders, rusted-through floorboard on the passenger side—you've probably seen in one or another family album, preserved in image if not in fact. After your grandparents updated to the '65 Galaxie, your dad drove the Falcon until, a gainfully employed college grad, he could afford a brand spanking new Austin-Healey in hunter green. Fabulous looking, but a lemon. I believe it was in the shop yet again the afternoon he met your mother, sent to pick up a prescription in her Mercedes 230SL. As a team your parents held titles to a Volkswagen van, a resourced cab, a Land Rover, and (also before your time) two Jeeps, one new, the other used, neither the red Jeep passed on to you.

Love,
Aunt K

DeeDee,

My favorite car memory isn't mine; it's your father's. And if memories were steal-able, I'd have thieved this: your dad drifting off to sleep after an exciting day at the beach in the backseat of George Grandy's fine Chrysler, that sedan packed and scrunched with three young couples and two tuckered sons, car windows rolled down, beachy smells mixing with tobacco and talc. In my elaboration: your dad's head rests in your grandmother's lap, his butt shoved up against your granddad's thigh, almost, almost asleep but still in some inner ear hearing: "Ya'll want this window up? Wind too much?" "Leave it, feels good—'less it's too much on you and Elsie?"

Nighty night,
Aunt K

West Coast
Thursday, May 16

DeeDee,

In a case of atrocious timing, my tenth-grade boyfriend and I broke up the week his parents bought him a baby blue Mustang. I won't pretend my head couldn't be turned by a fine set of wheels, but I wasn't *entirely* a car snob. Despite his GTO, I passed on a dance invite from a guy duller than lint. One can't converse with a car after all. Also: my last two years of high school, my replacement boyfriend (Larry B.) drove his dad's mail-delivery car, dented, gouged and scraped. Although we didn't further wreck that wreck, we did get in an accident together. To retrieve me and my suitcase overload from Governor's School, your grandparents lent Larry B. their Galaxie. On the way home, we crashed into another car, skidded into a ditch, got banged up but escaped serious injury—unlike the Galaxie, which was totaled. To replace it with the '68 Fairlane, your grandparents had to take on debt. Because they hadn't anticipated the need for a new car quite so soon, they'd put no car money aside. Phoning from the police station, Larry B. and I hadn't anticipated how little relieved we'd feel reporting that we were okay, though not the car. For your grandparents, debt was monstrously scary. They'd known so many who'd gone under, carrying it.

Love,
Aunt K

DeeDee,

It would make sense if I'd felt trapped in a car, *by* a car, as the Ford Galaxie veered toward the ditch or thereafter, surrounded by broken glass and crumpled metal. But it didn't happen then or then. It happened the afternoon cousin Linda and I had stayed late at school for a 4-H Club meeting, driven home by another club member's mom. Amped up on cookies and soda, we were a screechy gaggle of nine- and ten-year-olds cavorting on the backseat all the way home—or almost. As soon as Mrs. Simpson turned off East Ridge onto our dirt lane, we saw what shouldn't have been lined next to ditch cattails: car after truck after car, parked, drivers missing. As Linda shoved her way across legs, I frantically worked the door handle, Mrs. Simpson telling us to wait, just *wait*, until she'd come to a full stop. But we didn't wait. We'd run that dirt so many times for fun, for games, run it just to run and now we ran in terror toward Linda's house, streaked with black, still smoldering. The Meadses were okay; only the house had been harmed. But we hadn't known that, trapped in Mrs. Simpson's car. We weren't afforded that comfort, separated from our own.

Love,
Aunt K

West Coast
Sunday, May 19

DeeDee,

In my college luggage, I packed a caricature of Dustin Hoffman as Benjamin Braddock, an image that found a permanent home above my dorm room desk. My relationship with hometown honey Larry B. proved less enduring. By October, I'd moved on with, yep, a Dustin Hoffman look-alike driving a red Triumph convertible. Did the car attract more than the driver? It did. Do I fault any college girl for behaving like a shallow goof? I do not. (How many opportunities to play the goof does she get? Women have to man up long before men.) Back then I myself drove a yellow Pinto whose engine was expected to blow at 6,000 miles but lasted twenty times that. After any Saturday spent at home, I drove back to Chapel Hill on Sunday afternoon, travelling straight into the glare of a setting sun. The first two and a half hours of the trek consisted of secondary roads and small-town slowdowns, but on Interstate 85—then a mostly empty, cop-less highway—I got to floor it and with any luck managed to forget Monday, closing in. On my current six-lane Silicon Valley commute, I tend to obsess on how very little keeps drivers obeying the rules of the road given that people have bad days, *rotten* days (and nights) at the office, at the dentist's, in the company of mates/children/friends—major stuff happening in their heads, in their lives. Why trust any car to stay inside its lane at 80 miles per?

Love,
Aunt K

DeeDee,

Yes, your father and I have communicated. And, yes, your current mopey state regarding what to do next was mentioned. Let me be the first (or third?) to admit that, as a daughter, I overstayed my welcome, bunking with your grandparents, trading on their compulsory hospitality, taking monstrous advantage of their patience, their stocked refrigerator, and ready access to quality car repair at jury-rigger prices. But if you're reading this as my way of urging you to instantly leap into one or another something, please don't. I've expressed myself poorly. Let me try again. Waffling isn't necessarily a deplorable thing. Thrashing about helps sort which interests have the potential to stick, which are side trips, and which amount to feckless water treading. (And I speak as an expert waffler/thrasher/treader.) So what if it takes longer than the summer to plot your next great adventure? Neither of your parents will toss you out. And if they do, don't panic. Your aunt owns an air mattress.

Love,
Aunt K

DeeDee,

Whereas your grandmother preferred to annihilate copperheads and cottonmouths with a .22, the fat tires of a heavy-ass car were my weapons of choice, "smushed flat" my best assurance of snake FUBAR. *Far* less confident outside a vehicle, I constantly scanned the territory around my feet for slitherers. In retrospect, it's a distraction I sorely regret. I could have been observing so much else! In the backyard of your parents' starter house, above their makeshift hot tub, your mother strung an overhanging oak branch with lights; nature strung it with a snake that plopped into the hot tub with them one evening as they soaked. (Snakes dropping from trees: a disturbing *new* wrinkle in your aunt's universe.) Assuming *Gone with the Wind* didn't make it onto your high school reading list: spoiler alert. When little Wade Hamilton kills "a water moccasin all by himself" (page 135), that bold and brave act earns even Scarlett's grudging approval. The most proficient snake killers in our family were the women—no question. I'm ashamed to admit how long it took me to realize snuffing out vipers counted as the least of their braveries.

Love from rattlesnake country,
Aunt K

DeeDee,

Apologies. I went off on a snake jag when I should have stuck with the pups. No joke: reading any biography I first scan for canine references. Muriel Spark's Shadow. G. Stein's Basket I and II. ("I am because my little dog knows me.") Arthur Miller's Hugo. Marilyn Monroe's Josefa. If the too busy, too depressed, or too drugged-out Ms. Monroe neglected to walk Josefa, the Chihuahua relieved herself where she could, staining tony carpets. (What else was a dog to do?) In Rodmell, the Woolfs shared quarters with spaniels Pinka and the eczema-riddled Grizzle. While Leonard put in the training hours, Virginia holed up in her writing lodge composing Flush's dog's-eye view of the universe. The real Elizabeth Barrett Browning spaniel was snatched three times by dog thieves, who were three times paid off. Your parents' Newfoundland, Mercy, was also stolen three times by the same very reckless (or stupid) neighbor. The sheriff collected Mercy each time and brought him home, no ransom paid.

Love,
Aunt K

P.S. Thought for the week, courtesy of Joy Williams: "No man has ever died beside a sleeping dog."

DeeDee,

On the second floor of the Carolina building, above the Carolina Theatre, our family dentist drilled. In between cavity excavations, Dr. Johnson's patients could hear snatches of soundtrack, if not otherwise loopy on nitrous oxide. I hated going to the dentist. (Who doesn't?) I also had a mouthful of cavities, a situation that did nothing to improve my attitude. As a reward for getting through an exceptionally grueling session, your grandmother took me to see *Old Yeller*, downstairs. Since she hadn't read Fred Gipson's novel prior to (boy adopts dog; boy and dog bond; bad stuff befalls dog), she must have considered the Disney version a safe bet. (A very iffy post-*Bambi* assumption, it must be said.) When Old Yeller gets shot, I was by no means the only distraught child in the audience. However: judged by extremity of reaction, mine logged up there in the top five. Your grandmother quite literally had to drag me, bawling inconsolably, down the aisle toward daylight. During the car ride home, chest heaving with sobs, I assaulted the narrative. To spare Old Yeller's life, why couldn't *this* have happened, why couldn't *that*? An addiction, reworking the narrative. Once someone's developed a taste, does she ever go clear?

Love,
Aunt K

DeeDee,

Your parents' Caswell County house was surrounded by enough meadowland to justify acquiring a small John Deere for meadow mows (a "chore" your dad relished). The property, which also included a few derelict outbuildings, had been purchased by your other grandfather for investment purposes, and the straightforward arrangement he made with your parents was this: he'd pay for improvement materials but not the sweat equity. No objections from your parents who, as ever with house projects, jumped right in. Once they'd knocked down walls and opened up the kitchen and raised the ceiling in the main house, the space did feel airier and less cramped but it wouldn't have easily accommodated you—or any third occupant—even at the crib stage. Although your paternal grandparents were of the "animals belonged outside" persuasion, your mom and dad and I maintained an open-door pet policy that necessitated closing up shop every now and again and setting off flea bombs. Fallible devices, flea bombs. Ask your mom about the evening she returned to the scene wearing sandals. One stroll across the rug and her feet and ankles were peppered red with fleabites. I believe, on that occasion, your parents pitched a tent in the backyard and slept outside with the dogs, relying on better results from flea bomb number two.

And now I've made myself itch,
Aunt K

DeeDee,

Whenever your parents or I were away for any length of time (e.g., your parents' year in Spain), our dogs stayed on the farm with your grandparents. My dog, Shiloh, a lab and mystery mix, stayed longest. Each time I called home, your grandmother put the receiver to Shiloh's ear so I could talk to him also. During one of those phone conversations, your grandmother mentioned a cousin had stopped by, collecting for a clothing drive. After confirming she'd donated some of my left-behinds, your grandmother sighed. (Seldom welcome, what follows your grandmother's sigh.) The clothes rifling, window open, had sent wide my scent. Shiloh came running, thinking I'd returned. Unwilling to let that fact alone twist the knife, Cousin Myra wrote to say *she* could never leave a dog that loved her that much— never, ever. Cousin Myra and I have had our issues, but in this instance her criticism was bracingly just. I was still elsewhere when Shiloh was hit by a car and had to be put down. Your dad, in my stead, came home and stayed with him through the end. How much more can a sister ask of a brother?

Love,
Aunt K

RECREATORS WE.

DeeDee,

In the attic to this day: your dad's red and white baseball jersey
and green basketball warm-up pants. Before the moths found
it, my letter sweater also occupied an attic niche—though
less impressively. It had shrunk by half during a washing and
afterwards looked like something a five-year-old would consider
tight in the armpits. As my basketball player ID, I'd asked for
number fifteen solely because it had been your dad's jersey
number. Alas, my team didn't get to retire our jerseys once
we graduated. Number fifteen carried on without me. (Shared
athletic wear. Can't say I'm a fan.) For four semesters of required
(yes, *required*) PE in college, we gals flung off jeans and crocheted
shawls to speed-change into shapeless snap-on onesies, never the
same onesie twice. Every freshman and sophomore, male and
female, expected to get an A in PE because who doesn't ace PE,
right? Your aunt. Not once in four semesters. Your grandparents,
probably the only parents on earth who sent a kid to college with
instructions not to "wear herself out studying," blinked at those
Phys Ed Bs as well. They never assumed they'd raised a scholar,
but an inferior athlete? That judgment hurt their pride.

Love,
Aunt K

West Coast
Sunday, June 2

DeeDee,

When did I bring up faulty eyesight? Last month? Despite the impediment, neither your dad nor I wore glasses while playing sports. I can't speak to his reasons but mine were straightforward: clarity screwed up my aim and catch. The captain of my basketball team also needed help in the vision department but preferred contacts to glasses. When rebound knockabouts sent one of her blue-tinted lenses flying, the ref called time and we dropped to our knees in search of what we (amazingly) always found. Your dad passed on sticking glass in his eye; I briefly succumbed to the temptation. In the optometrist's opinion, if I wore a single lens, the vision in my other eye would "adjust." Playing the sheet-covered corpse in the school play that year, I blinked wrong during a performance, causing my lone contact to wander—an uncorrectable mishap in the moment since my dead character wasn't scripted to rise. By the time the curtain fell, my eye was a mess: red, watery, supremely tender to the touch. It took another quarter hour of gouging to liberate the lens from my lower eyelid, after which my contact lens and I parted company evermore. When you were at the babyhood stage of staring unrepentantly at oddities, you used to stare long and hard (for good cause) at my ginormous goggle-style glasses. Whatever was I thinking? A more hideous frame for the close-eyed has yet to be invented.

Love,
Aunt K

DeeDee,

I assume by your era high schools had dispensed with herding students into the gym to take the Armed Services Vocational Aptitude Battery test. (Correct me if I'm mistaken.) Your dad says he doesn't remember taking any standardized tests—but that's just to get my goat. Since my classroom performance was respectable, my consistently low scores on anything billed as an achievement test perplexed teachers who, by sharing their perplexity, put your grandparents on notice to fret as well. Cross-examined, I had no concrete excuses—something about those ready-set-go question packets just threw me off my stride. So when my ASVAB results rolled in, previously concerned adults expressed relief. If every other career path failed me, I could join the army. The reason I tested better on the ASVAB? The space perception section. Shapes I could fit together. What that minor talent seems to facilitate in the day-to-day: no measuring necessary before heaving a bookshelf into a cranny with a quarter-inch, either side, to spare. Less helpful offshoot: I have a clearer memory of where people stood during a conversation than what they said. All this to say: if *your* brain prioritizes content over placement, you've every cause to feel pleased and no cause to worry. What good is a "measuring" eye, really? Parlor trick, more or less.

Love,
Aunt K

DeeDee,

For my eleventh birthday celebration, your granddad put together a high jump and gave over one of his bamboo fishing poles for the lath. Quite the party hit! I'd just fallen on my ass, taking the pole down with me, when your grandmother emerged from the kitchen to distribute more chips. Trying her luck, she cleared the pole with a nifty scissor-leg maneuver. On the face of it: a mother bested her daughter at her daughter's b-day party. I suppose I could have felt put out but, as were my pals, I was impressed. She'd cleared her mark with a full inch to spare. Start to finish, the family's position on athletic competition was uncomplicated, un-agonized and unsparing. "Holding back" because another relative was in the race? Ludicrous. How one acted as a champ required a different set of ethics. When your dad, a junior, received the All-Sports Award historically awarded to a graduating senior, your grandparents and I were as stunned as the rest of the commencement crowd. Also *ecstatic*—but careful to contain our glee lest it be mistaken for grandiosity. Your dad had the harder job of accepting glory without rubbing it in, which he pulled off, solemnly shaking the coach's hand. There's a photo of him in shiny suit and peg-legged pants coming offstage, head slightly bowed. The bunch of us waited for the car ride home to celebrate. And then we let loose—oh my we did.

Love,
Aunt K

DeeDee,

Two other examples of your dad's charmed (sporting) life. Practicing catch inside a chock-full-of-antiques house, he threw a curveball his pal Lucian missed and one of a pair of matching lamps caught. Alerted by the sound of breaking glass, Lucian's mom, Evelyn, came downstairs to survey the damage. Contrite and terrified, your dad confessed at once. After a moment's silence, Evelyn told both guys to "clean up their mess," left them to it, returned to her business upstairs and that was that. A few years later, throwing for the out, pitcher's mound to first base, your dad threw high and broke the first baseman's nose. Bloodied, Fred E.'s honker—no vision to behold in its natural state—looked not only unattractive but unsalvageable. Misery times two: Fred E. had to sit out the rest of the game. Of course your dad was sorry. Of course there were those (ahem) who argued the fault lay not with the pitcher but with the wounded, who hadn't sufficiently raised his glove. Nonetheless, a broken nose is a broken nose, hard to forgive or forget. And yet, Fred E. never held his broken nose against your dad, steadfast in his friendship throughout baseball season and beyond.

Love,
Aunt K

DeeDee,

At least within recent memory (your dad's and my own), none of the clan went in for solitary athletic endeavors—no long-distance runners, no solo mountaineers among us. We championed team sweats because if it's just you in the game, yourself playing yourself, who's there to rag and rival, yeah? Your granddad, like your dad, was a baseball standout and, also like your dad, a starting pitcher. As a lefty himself, teaching his right-handed children to throw and hit required ambidextrous grace. Your grandmother played basketball when uniforms were individually assembled. For her '35 Moyock High team she competed in white turtleneck and shorts, but didn't, like her co captain, wear a cloche. In Hatteras, twice, she played on a drifting outdoor court. Can you fathom? Trying to dribble on sand? My first pair of high-tops, worn slick by an older cousin, proved useless against Griggs Elementary and a polished linoleum court. No tread, no traction. During four long quarters of slip-sliding and colliding, I committed three fouls, picked up twelve travelling violations, and scored a single basket—and that conversion *only* after I'd given up the dream of layups.

Currently without a BB goal,
Aunt K

DeeDee,

I think it's fair to say croquet never counted as a contender for favorite family sport, but when we did play we played on a flat-ish section of weedy yard between the cousins' houses, Sunday afternoon. Your grandfather used his extra turns to knock wide the competition's ball, even on those occasions when his whiny girl child begged for clemency. *Them's the breaks, kid!* Tennis, however, we all took up with a vengeance, the former croquet "lawn" transformed into a 36' x 78' dirt court with roots. Scrupulously fair, your grandparents purchased tennis racquets for both their (unequally skilled) children and, for their own game sets, borrowed equipment from us. Word got around. Community folks who didn't strictly count as buddies started showing up to practice their swings with our tennis balls. So my (true) buddy Shirley and I, chauffeured by her mom, switched over to E. City's no-shade asphalt courts. More often than not we finished the set before the lure of cheeseburgers and orangeades caused us to pack it in. But, you know, we were just goofing around, no one watching but Shirley's mom and she only now and again, glancing up from her movie mag. If it had been *official*, a real regulation match, we'd have suffered sunstroke before quitting.

Love,
Aunt K

West Coast
Saturday, June 15

DeeDee,

The same Shirley and I bowled for three years in a Saturday morning league, suited up in navy shorts and white blouses stitched with orange Culpepper Hardware logos. To secure that business sponsorship, we had to convince Mr. Culpepper that shelling out for our team's three games each Saturday, in addition to the up-front expense of the felt logos, served his business interests. While Shirley argued our case—we were *the* best team, a shoo-in for trophy honors—I strove to appear qualm-free. (The youngest bowler on our team threw two-handed from the foul line and seldom managed a slo-mo strike.) Mr. Culpepper listened with sleepy eyes but in the end wrote out a check. The owner of the bowling alley, another sleepy-eyed fellow, took Mr. Culpepper's cash from us, handed out bowling shoes and spoke not a word. (Hangover sufferer, I'd guess now.) In her methodical, melancholy way, his wife, Mrs. D., helped all of us improve our games. We loved her unconditionally. I also developed a mad crush on the boy who lived next door and sporadically came in to roll a few. Very loud, bowling alleys. To share with Shirley the news that HE was IN THE BUILDING, I had to shout, risking humiliation on multiple fronts. Never acknowledged my existence, that fellow. Unrequited like and gutter balls.

Love,
Aunt K

DeeDee,

Also appearing in the unrequited column: my febrile lust for the fellow across the aisle in Russian History 31. He was long and lean and darkly handsome and appeared to also darkly brood— dark, mysterious brooding (or what I took for it), a tried and true aphrodisiac for your aunt. (Though, in this case, the object of my desire was more likely a stoner than a brooder.) End of semester, I thought he'd disappeared into the campus hordes and escaped my radar, but his girlfriend was a friend of a friend, so info trickled in. The girlfriend had him on a tight leash. One of the reasons he stayed long and lean: if he gained a pound, the girlfriend demanded he snort coke until he dropped that bugger. Also, on her command, they clocked in two hours of yoga daily—which might well have served as her aphrodisiac. In sum, the fellow was utterly taken and thoroughly monitored. Given such conditions and restrictions—even if I'd embraced yoga—difficult to get a flirt in.

Love,
Aunt K

DeeDee,

Music and lust—there's a dyad. But just now I'm thinking more in terms of musical transactions, as in your dad and two of our first cousins convening on the living room rug to bargain and swap 45 rpm vinyl. Such negotiations weren't for the timid. Any disputes regarding scratch-and-warp were conclusively settled by a spin on our Zenith console. I was allowed on the outskirts but given no vote, a painful exclusion when your dad's copies of "Bye, Bye, Love" and the Isley Brothers' "Twist and Shout" went up for grabs. The Zenith saw both of us through high school, much to the fury of your great-grandmother, who complained she could hear "that racket clear across the field." I added to her ire by playing the same record (Little Eva's "Locomotion") incessantly. But why not listen ad nauseam if you love a song? Neither your dad nor I treated our 45s anything like gently. Singles got sat on; jackets went missing. What didn't break or get traded eventually ended up in the attic, stuck together, melting from heat. You'd think that neglect signaled musical indifference, but no. We'd just moved on to 33s.

Love,
Aunt K

West Coast
Wednesday, June 19

DeeDee,

I sent last week—not to you—a postcard of Elvis Presley's 845 West Chino Canyon Road abode in Palm Springs. The house is a sprawler though not, in the sum of its parts, all that impressive. Standard-issue stucco walls, red tile roof and, unlike at Graceland, no musical notes embellishing the gate. If he'd been a golfer-slash-insurance salesman, Elvis would have fit into the neighborhood just swell. While driving past and rubbernecking the actual compound, I flashed on pal Shirley and I performing "G. I. Blues" at a church social. Preparing, we'd had enormous trouble deciphering some of the lyrics. (And we, Southern gals!) Never having heard of the "Rhine," but well-acquainted with amusement parks, we assumed Elvis viewed a "beautiful ride." That's funny, right? (Or would be if you knew what in God's name I was referencing.) Before it became the norm to include song lyrics on record albums, I regularly misheard/rewrote lyrics. Until very recently I thought Joni Mitchell sang that hell was a hippie's way to go out—which, post-'68, seemed as true a prediction as any. Even at that sputtering-of-an-era date, I'd have liked to have qualified as a member of Hippy Nation. I had the long, flowing hair. And your grandmother had stitched up any number of maxi frocks with empire waists and billowing sleeves that I wore with pride if not distinction. It was the mellow element of the profile that eluded me. Still does.

Hup two three four,
Aunt K

DeeDee,

To rib your father, ask him about his black patent leather tap shoes. Back when, searching for something else entirely (croquet mallet? tennis ball?), I chanced upon those "dancers" beneath a mound of fraying sneakers in the hallway closet. (Spiders found them first.) This much I pried out of your grandmother: when two of the girl cousins signed up for lessons, your grandmother, not wishing your father, age six, to miss out on "enrichment," signed him up also. Whatever happened at those sessions—and your father remains mum—I'm inclined to blame the experience for his subsequent lack of dance enthusiasm. Perhaps you'll be able to get to the bottom of the mystery. If so, share?

Love,
Aunt K

DeeDee,

Your grandmother, watching TV, used to lend her arm for me to yank about while I danced the bop. At some point, because of the wrenching or because she wanted her arm back, string looped around a doorknob served as my partner. In the earliest home movies, I twirl and twist for the camera, having fun, showing off. Then came a growth spurt, self-consciousness, frame after frame of me squirreled away in corners, face averted, shoulders hunched, victim of some traumatic body snatch. Although I don't recall any filmic immortalization of your bottled-up misery, there is a video of you ferociously kicking a fence. Fortunately you grew out of tantrums and my dancing revived with the assistance of terrific hoofer Larry B. Together he and I worked out an elaborate routine to preview among the Casino's elbow-to-elbow Saturday crowd, our daily practice sessions rewarded the night a total stranger ran up to our sweatiness and gushed compliments. Later, Larry B. and I enjoyed a certain notoriety for slow dancing to the Showmen's "39-21-40 Shape," your aunt's debilitating self-consciousness apparently in remission.

Love,
Aunt K

DeeDee,

Before we hooked up, Larry B. dated the enviable Christine, she of the low-pitched, gravelly voice and white-blonde locks, sole female in a rock band that performed across three counties. She could be a bitch but had the license to be (to repeat: she *sang in a band*), so no one truly held it against her when she gave herself airs. Despite her limited vocal range, her solos of "Stand By Me" and "96 Tears" did those songs proud. Like her bandmates, Christine's onstage outfit consisted of a white shirt, black vest, black slacks and black tie. Androgyny suited her. In her twenties she became a nurse, married a doctor. Surely she kept scrapbooks? Surely some cozy night at the beach house, in front of a roaring fire, she revived one of her old standards, minus the Oxford shirt, for the hubby? When a rock 'n' roll gal quits the biz, is it with sorrow or relief? I was never tight with Christine; she didn't confide in me then and wouldn't, on demand, divulge those details now. All very disappointing. And you, darling niece? Does the enormity of what you wish you knew but never shall, big stuff to piddling, dispirit? I hope not; I hope not yet.

Love,
Aunt K

DeeDee,

Why two notes in one day? Pre-midnight memory of an eighth-grade talent contest featuring baton twirlers, piano pounders, and two separate renditions of "You'll Never Walk Alone." The surprise entrants: cousins Diane and Frieda Banks, who sang over the Crystals singing "Da Doo Ron Ron." Decked out in voluminous skirts, shiny belts cinched tight, Diane and Frieda performed with panache, and they were good, exceptionally good, for our little nothing of a show. Not that talent actually mattered. Only popularity counted—which the Banks cousins knew going in and still gutsily went ahead with their act, putting themselves out there to be judged by a smug, already-decided audience. Once they finished, applause was weak, scattered. A pointedly tepid response. Regardless—and this is the part of the memory with the sharpest teeth—Frieda and Diane looked well pleased with themselves, thoroughly satisfied with what they'd accomplished. As they bowed, they squeezed hands, grinned at each other. Sitting down to write this second dispatch, I didn't realize I'd be reanimating occasions about which to feel ashamed or describing cruelty and courage and how often the two conflate. But such is the consequence.

Love,
Aunt K

DeeDee,

And now I'm remembering a stretch of post-college nights that started with dancing and ended in punches thrown by the many or the few. Someone bumped into someone else who was sleeping with another someone the first someone wanted to be sleeping with and the second someone couldn't let that act of aggression go unchallenged and on from there. A dog pile of testosterone. It rekindled my dance phobia for a while, that dick demo, because once bouncers are involved, where's the fun? Then again, I was never the someone fought over, so perhaps exclusion colored my judgment. Nothing explains why or how I managed to live for so long with a dance refusenik. Equally puzzling: how he lived with me, recreational discord rather low on our list of incompatibilities. Your dad and mom, consistently friendly to whomever I dragged through the door, behaved in their usual cordial manner to his drag-in, but their dogs at the time, Swampy and Sundance, felt less compelled to welcome a stranger into our midst. A difficult evening it was, that get-to-know dinner. Your contribution: puking up applesauce. Belated thanks. It was a diversion desperately needed.

Love,
Aunt K

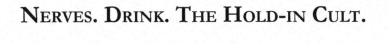

NERVES. DRINK. THE HOLD-IN CULT.

West Coast
Monday, July 1

DeeDee,

Occasionally your grandmother would declare herself "in a strain." One circumstance that provoked that malady: having to roll out the hospitality mat with little in the cupboard. To appreciate this story, you'll have to cast your mind back to the (barely conceivable) time and place of your father's and my childhood in a neighborhood where telephones were rare. If and when folks felt the urge to visit, they piled in the car and showed up on the doorstep unannounced, often near the dinner hour. "In a strain," your grandmother then attempted to feed eight on one fried chicken without making any serving appear, God forbid, skimpy. Glancing up to see the relatives from Hampton Roads, we knew we were in for overnight as well as dinner guests because "what would be the sense of driving an hour to stay less than twelve?" On those occasions, your grandmother—in a *decided* strain—tore around the house, snatching up clutter, offering iced tea, assuring her brother and family their sleepover caused "no trouble whatsoever." Meanwhile, I skulked near the trunk of the visitors' Oldsmobile Deluxe. Whenever my Hampton Roads cousin tired of a toy, I benefited. Which is to say, in my all-consuming self-centeredness, I remained totally oblivious to your grandmother's strain. May your own children prove more considerate.

Love,
Aunt K

DeeDee,

During one of my "back home for a spell" stretches, a carload of aunts and female cousins took in a Sunday matinee of *Crimes of the Heart*. One long row of Southern women straw-sipping Pepsi, crunching butter-soaked popcorn, settled in to watch a Southern tale that had been filmed "just down the coast" in Southport. The movie version, as well it should have, preserved the play's pivotal scenes and lines, notably the Meg and Babe variations of having a "bad day." A real bad day. I'm prepared to swear that every relation to my right and left nodded when Jessica Lange offered her bad-day summary and again, near movie's end, when Sissy Spacek mouthed the same. My head also bobbed—a tad too vigorously for your grandmother's taste. However much your grandmother agreed with the sentiment, she detested blatant display. One of our tensions, your grandmother's and mine (even when we didn't lodge under the same roof): degree of reveal.

Love from the family tell-all,
Aunt K

DeeDee,

When our neighbor down the road, Lucille S., discovered a lump in her breast, she told no one, terrified of hospitals. (Miss Lucille's mother died in one.) For several years Miss Lucille successfully kept her health secret, secret. Then one day Miss Lucille's daughter dropped by for a visit and found her mother screaming "at the walls," experiencing what was thereafter labeled "a fit of nerves." Because Miss Lucille's daughter and son, summoned from the cornfield, together failed to calm their mother, they phoned the rescue squad. Sedated, Miss Lucille was delivered to the E. City hospital. Once the sedation wore off, Miss Lucille jumped out of the hospital's second storey window, broke her leg, and was dragging herself toward the perimeter's boxwood shrubs when retrieved, sedated more heavily and transferred to the psychiatric ward at Norfolk General. Over the months that followed, whenever that sequence of happenings got chewed on and over, a community commentator, summing up for the group, closed down the discussion with: "She started screaming, you see." As if screaming were the sole cause of mishap. Not the cancer, not the depression: the screaming.

Love,
Aunt K

DeeDee,

An intra-familial "nerves" example: Uncle Howard often cried at supper tables. At one such supper table, I bore witness. Your grandmother had cooked a pot roast for her youngest brother's visit, and your grandfather, in deference to our guest, had double-scrubbed his knuckles with Borax before sitting down to eat. Your dad wasn't there, which was unfortunate, his absence robbing me of the reaction of a near-contemporary to emulate. Purely by happenstance, I was the first to notice the rolling tears as well as Uncle Howard's striking posture: a kind of paralyzed uprightness, as if rigidity would dry the drip. Finally your grandmother said, with feeling, "Oh, Howard!" After which three of us put down our forks and waited, still and speechless, as if our strict containment would help Uncle Howard recover his. Despite your dad's having missed suppertime with Uncle Howard, he was well-acquainted with standard operating policy. We might have been non-rabid Baptists, but holding in remained an unshakeable tenant of faith. Those tantrums of yours I referenced earlier? Their uninterrupted playout? Credit your dad's distaste for the cult of hold-in.

Love,
Aunt K

West Coast
Saturday, July 6

DeeDee,

Before she married, one of your paternal great-aunts worked for a year at Dix Hill in Raleigh. (Because "Dix Hill" was used interchangeably with "nuthouse," having an aunt work there, as opposed to being sent there, was considered a dual blessing.) I believe Aunt Dora worked as a nursing assistant, but I could be wrong about the payroll classification. Beyond dispute: any training she received, she received on the job; she didn't have a nursing degree. What she did have going for her: considerable strength for a woman her size and an unexcitable nature—both assets, one presumes, when interacting with the mentally unstable. Although our eighth-grade history text covered Dorothea Dix's pioneering social reforms, her volunteer service as the Union's Superintendent of Female Nurses following the battle of Fort Sumter was nowhere mentioned. (Hmm.) Another suspicious Dorothea Dix exclusion: on our field trip to Raleigh, my psych class didn't, as might be predicted, congregate in the lobby of her namesake hospital. Instead, we collegians were funneled into Central Prison to gawp at the state's execution chamber, temporarily in disuse. Oversized, wooden and severely straight-backed, the state's lethal chair. Construction materials, joinery angles—those the details I remember. A case of the eye fixing on what it could bear, I suppose. The eye and the mind.

Love,
Aunt K

DeeDee,

In my first-round V. Woolf infatuation, I came across a photo of the author leaning against a stone doorway, right hand stuck in the pocket of one of many layers of clothing, left hand crooked and rising toward her chin, right foot kicked back behind her. Very likely you've seen the photograph—it's now everywhere published. New to my eyes, the most riveting aspect of the image, besides its seeming informality, was Woolf's tilted head and facial expression. I made a photocopy because I thought it captured the writer in one of her mad/near-mad moments and eerily conveyed the essence of that mind state—off-kilter, vulnerable, ever so slightly on guard. I was wrong, of course. The photo was taken at Knole, Vita Sackville-West's ancestral digs. And it wasn't a visual of Virginia mad; it was a visual of Virginia in love.

Hugs,
Aunt K

DeeDee,

Confessional poets—and, let's be honest, the suicides of confessional poets—turned a sizeable chunk of your aunt's college contemporaries into anguished romantics. The fragmented self's fragmentations exhaustively examined. Psychic wounds flagrantly exposed. Such unabashed, unashamed and uncensored revealing left us awestruck—and envious. But whereas self-evisceration on the page came off empowering, in life mode that kind of sensibility got folks ostracized, hospitalized, electroshocked, and dismissed as functioning members of the body politic. Regardless, before we aged out, awe carried the day. And what has any of this to do with your kin? Not much, except as illustration of the path not taken. However miserable the living, none in our family seem to have opted to speed the finale. Our collective MO tracks more ornery—and more resigned. In the face of failure and disappointment, disaster and heartbreak, the Meadses, as one non-relation put it, "set their jaws and hunker down."

Love,
Aunt K

West Coast
Wednesday, July 10

DeeDee,

Have you run across the explanation of what separates a novel of detection from a novel of suspense? The "pure" detective story gazing/spiraling backward, focused on the past and what happened therein, the suspense narrative another can of worms altogether: imperiled characters propelled toward an unknowable, more threatening future. Remarkable—isn't it?—that we (even *as readers*) can stomach the suspense formula, criminals seldom apprehended, justice in short supply, control an illusion, any escape from chaos and danger a temporary reprieve for ever/ always around the next corner and curve: more chaos, more danger, the comforts of salvation, and closure denied. What set me going on genre distinctions this starry evening while lolling al fresco in my Adirondack chair was fate and how difficult it seems for Southerners to relinquish investment in the controlling idea of. In a community as tiny as the one your dad and I grew up in, generational patterns and their damage were impossible to disregard. Complicating that complication: the fatalistically inclined's tendency to assign blame elsewhere, be it bad luck or iffy heritage. What I've since come to understand is how easily the fate card operates as justification and excuse, a rationale for shucking off responsibility, for allowing the continuance of scarring harm, for flaunting a hardwired resistance to change. Since sobering wasn't my aim, not the best of topics to contemplate, drink in hand.

Love,
Aunt K

DeeDee,

After she drowned, two pairs of Virginia Woolf's "tortoiseshell spectacles" were auctioned off by Sotheby's for 250 and 260 pounds, respectively. Eyeglasses are as personal as underwear, if you think about it, but unnecessary for one who knows her way to the water's edge. The New York Public Library owns the walking stick she took with her to the River Ouse. Depending on which biography you read, it went with her into the water and later washed ashore or she left it on the riverbank. To take it with her made it part of the disappearance; to leave it behind announced the departure. A major difference in intent, it seems to me. To avoid sprinkling Woolfian references throughout, why don't I bundle here? For reasons not all dreadful, you'll be hard pressed to appreciate Woolf's soaring importance to my crowd of college femmes, but *try*. At the time *very* few female authors slipped past the academic barricades and landed on a syllabus, and we bonded mightily to those who managed the feat. One semester I impetuously attempted a paper on Woolf's fiction. A single paper! On all her fiction! Such lunacy! But those weeks of reading her words morning, noon, and night? Divine.

Love,
Aunt K

West Coast
Friday, July 12

DeeDee,

Two food and drink recommendations should you find yourself
travelling New Mexico's Highway 25. Make a pit stop at The
Range in Bernalillo and order chicken salad—the tastiest, bar
none, your aunt has swallowed west of the Mississippi. Tangy,
not soupy. (Your grandmother would approve.) Also for sale
onsite: an enthralling cache of postcards, though I passed on a
facial composite of 1,000 meth addicts. Once in the vicinity of
Santa Fe, override your tourist trap misgivings, start scanning for
a parking spot a mile or so from the Plaza and hoof it the rest
of the way to the La Fonda Hotel bar. *Excellent* vodka martinis,
served at mostly any hour of the day and night. Plus you'll be
drinking with the knowledge that on these premises a restless
Kitty Oppenheimer tossed back a few, having made the thirty-
five-mile journey from Los Alamos whenever the hell she felt
like it, gas rationing be damned. A dissatisfied wife, yes, but also
bodily lucky. Negotiating that mountain grade fifty years later on
a vastly improved road surface, stone cold sober, can be plenty
dicey. If you decide to take in Los Alamos as well, avoid doing
so on a tight schedule. It's a layered place—atmospherically,
historically. But, then again, I'm of an age susceptible to its
spookiness. Georgia O'Keeffe's fallout shelter in Abiquiu? Did
I mention?

Love,
Aunt K

DeeDee,

It was also in Bernalillo (town of the delicious chicken salad) that Sam Shepard's father was knocked down and killed by a car when he stepped backward into traffic following a lengthy sit-stay at the bar. Also, according to the playwright: during a performance of *Buried Child*, his inebriated dad rose from the audience to dispute the stage version's version of events, shouting at the actors and flailing his fists. Though less boisterous, our family's methods of disputing contrary accounts of the truth still come across loud and clear. If, for instance, my letters to you landed on your grandmother's porch for a read-through in the presence of one of your great-aunts, the scene would play out thus: a moment of strategic silence, nonexistent lint flicked kneecap to porch board, delicate and unnecessary throat clearings—all prelude to the first pitying snipe. "We all remember things differently, I suppose," the *suppose* a sop to your grandmother, unfortunate birth agent of the taleteller who "didn't get it right." Should your grandmother remain noncommittal, your emboldened great-aunt might risk extending censure's range to the tune of: "She always exaggerated, even as a child." In such circumstances, would your grandmother continue to keep her counsel, allow the double-barreled rebuke of her child to stand unchallenged? Possibly— since she, herself, considers exaggeration my greatest flaw.

Love,
Aunt K

DeeDee,

Your aunt's *own* first serious attack of the willies—which I'll take pains to *understate* here—occurred on the eve of a high school history exam, sophomore year. Strangely (or part of the strangeness): I didn't really need to study, not in the painstakingly detailed way that I did, starting around 11:30 p.m. or so. Other humans inside the house and various pets outside it had already found their way to dreamland; only I fought off the Sandman. Around midnight, I began to notice/overly notice the baseboard heater knocking on and off. Soon thereafter I started flipping between the pages I'd reviewed and those I still needed to review. Back and forth and back and forth. Then the thumb marking my reading line began to tremble in unprecedented fashion. Then my chest tightened. Then breathing became less deep dive than surface pant. All in all, symptoms of a fairly classic anxiety attack and, in this instance, pigheadedly self-orchestrated. In the years since, which state of being has felt worse to me in situ: anxious jitters or benumbed lethargy? Lethargy. I'd much rather go sleepless from worry shakes than feel incapable of rising from bed to brush my teeth. (Not that I expect preferences to hold sway.)

Love,
Aunt K

DeeDee,

Despite what you might have heard, I did *not* paint *everything* in my New York apartment green, just the floors—and I'd do the same again. It was a comfort for a country gal, after trudging concrete, to spy some green underfoot, even if that green didn't oscillate or tickle. I fit none of E.B. White's categories for NYC residents: native, commuter, or settler who'd come "in search of something." I'd just come because it was somewhere I hadn't been. Predictably (given my origin story), the compacting of people and real estate unsettled me. At the sight of a high-rise apartment building, I'd fall into an apprehensive trance, overwhelmed by the sheer number of human dramas being played out on a moment-to-moment basis behind those banks of windows, the immensity of the aggregate, the inescapable awareness of so many unknowable mysteries and lives. (A ruralite's response in every way.) At some fundamental, emotional level, I felt both dogged and over-stimulated by urban life. I also sensed, lurking, too many opportunities to exist disappeared. Despite working at the best paying job I'd had up to that point, I quickly realized I wasn't long for the set-up. Understand: I'm not contending that you or anyone "from the sticks" can't turn into a bona fide city creature. My bowling buddy Shirley, for instance, took to Manhattan like a frog to a pond and lives there still: a mom and a Wall Street lawyer.

Love,
Aunt K

DeeDee,

At the tail end of my NYC adventure, at a literary-ish dinner party, someone insisted everyone declare her or his "favorite novel of all time." Perennial favorite *Heart of Darkness* collected votes right and left because who ever goes wrong extolling Conrad? I didn't then and don't now have an *all-time favorite* novel—why narrow what needn't be narrowed?—and, frankly, I resented the probe. To avoid contributing to the conversation/inquisition, I tried various deflection tactics (lowered eyelids, hearty forking, mouth stuffed to the max), all of which succeeded in calling more, not less, attention to my opt out. Bullied, your aunt typically (and most often unwisely) defaults to sarcasm. No way in hell was I going to cough up the name of a book not written by a Southerner. The novel that proclaimed "Nobody but a Southerner knows the wrenching rinsing sadness of the cities of the North" seemed as good a riposte as any. Afterwards, though, I felt contrite and embarrassed. A book as fine as *The Moviegoer* shouldn't be called into service simply to even a score.

Love,
Aunt K

West Coast
Wednesday, July 17

DeeDee,

As recently as last month, I nearly came to blows with a complete stranger. Here's why. The actress Gena Rowlands had journeyed from Los Angeles to discuss *Woman Under the Influence* at a Tenderloin fundraiser, her wondrous self agreeing to appear onstage, "in the flesh," to answer audience questions following the showing. As the house lights dimmed, a late-arriving someone (your age, I fear) plopped into the seat beside me and inquired: "So what's this movie about, anyway?" Nonchalant ignorance. So very, very galling. As if that sacrilege weren't enough: movie playing, my row mate wiggled restlessly throughout the *mesmerizing* scene of Mabel freaking out as she waits for her kids' school bus. I mean *really*. *Never* let me hear comparable tales about *your* indifference to Ms. Rowlands's artistry. I simply couldn't bear the mortification of association. In addition, in my presence, refrain from making snide asides about Chloe Webb's "What about the farewell drugs?" speech in *Sid and Nancy*. Although I may be the only person you know—or will know—who twelve times paid to see that colossally depressing film, keep in mind the context: in the Seventies and Eighties, depressing played extremely well.

Love,
Aunt K

DeeDee,

Thumbtack-ed to the corkboard directly across from where I type: xeroxed images of Anna Akhmatova, George Eliot, Mary Tormented Lincoln, Cindy Sherman as Lucille Ball, Wallis from Baltimore Simpson. Surrounding those visuals, word thefts: "That plastic smile people wear when they are trying not to scream." (Raymond Chandler) "It is awfully hard for anyone to go on doing anything because everybody is troubled by everything." (Gertrude Stein) "I wanted to jump, but I did not jump." (Angela Carter) "Hanging on to dreams is like trying to eat a smell." (Robert Coover) "Yes, always someone dies." (Stevie Smith) A collection of sad-eyed portraits—even Cindy's Lucy, even Wallis—and declarations tinged with melancholia. Was it always so of your aunt's bulletin board selections? Probably. Would such flashpoints stashed away in a file or cabinet drawer denote equilibrium (achieved)? Probably not. The out of sight/ out of mind argument doesn't hold water for farmers' daughters.

Love,
Aunt K

DeeDee,

Your grandmother's best friend grew up in Old Trap, a settlement that took its name from a tavern that "lured men from home and held them." Old Trap was a quick run from your grandparents' house, a straight shot down Indiantown Road. As visiting adults, both your dad and I regularly wished that 1800s tavern continued to serve. Within striking distance of our base camp, we'd have proved loyal customers (maybe a little *too* loyal). Drinking to pass the time, drinking to get through, drinking to drink. Never a shortage of reasons to imbibe. In terms of heritage: your great-uncle Monford was, to my knowledge, the only confirmed drunk on our side of the fence. Meaning: Uncle Monford drank regularly, to excess, and didn't try to cover up that he drank regularly, to excess. He went about his drinking forthrightly, appalled relatives be damned and died in a car crash, driving while (presumably) drunk. Driving drunk didn't that often turn into a death sentence in his era because county roads were lightly travelled. They were still relatively lightly travelled when your dad and I were old enough to cruise about on Saturday nights. But because I'm now middle-aged and more easily daunted, I dislike remembering how often we and every friend we had left the beach, crossed a rickety bridge, and sped through swampland, over-served by Casino staff. No one was ever carded. No one was judged "over the limit." And no one got a ticket for driving impaired. Once Larry B. and I did get pulled over because of his weaving, but the officer who stopped us allowed me, wearing Larry B.'s specs, to take the wheel and the pair of us to motor on.

Love,
Aunt K

DeeDee,

It ventures into chicken or egg territory, doesn't it? Drinking, the blues/the blues, drinking. The most unhappy I've felt start-to-finish drinking was at a rum and Coke sendoff party for a Vietnam War draftee. An unhappiness no less intense but more gradual in onslaught: day drinking with someone I still cared for at the end of a rocky romance. There was the night your dad overindulged and broke his ankle. There was that period when your mom liked to close down the bars in town. And, yes, there's nothing more tedious that other people's drinking and drugging stories. Having put in more time with alcohol, I'm better acquainted with the satisfactions and dissatisfactions of numbness versus euphoria. Our chunk of you is more inclined toward depression than dipsomania, if a three-generation poll can be trusted. Why so, I wonder? The difficulty of acquiring moonshine? No ABC store open after midnight? Less of a hassle to go with ineffably sad? When inquiring mind V.S. Naipaul asked, Georgia-born Anne Siddons told: "There are many drunk women in the South." In the opinion of someone currently perched on a Western fault line: not all such women reside in the South.

Love,
Aunt K

West Coast,
Wednesday, July 31

DeeDee,

Although we both thought I'd done with the subject of drinking/ the urge to do so, evidence in hand suggests otherwise. The excuse: on my lunch break today, either by chance or cosmic directive, your aunt received a prod. Browsing the library's biography shelves what did I come upon but a paragraph dissecting the drinking patterns of novelist Elizabeth Bowen. I should have scribbled the entire passage of what Bowen's contemporaries had to say about the matter for fullest effect here, but since I didn't, I'll go with what I can recall: "There was no suggestion that she ever became drunk." Meant as high praise, you understand. In your aunt's experience, men who get smashed, get smashed with the expectation that they will, once sober, be excused and possibly applauded for any spectacle they made of themselves during the bender and forgiven for any harm(s) done. On those occasions when women let rip, more often than not we wake personally chagrined with certain knowledge of having been collectively sneered at. An unfair distribution of effects. Or do I (again) wax redundant?

Love,
Aunt K

AUGUST NOTES

[Missing/presumed lost]

MONTHLIES. MATRIMONIES.

DeeDee,

On this the family agreed: the gift giver with the most cash and clout among us was your great-aunt Vivian. Cash because of her extra-income civil service job, clout because of her inspired and (relatively) pricey presents. What I most needed my pre-college summer from Aunt Vivian—and from any other generous soul who'd pitch in—were unencumbered funds. Instead Aunt Vivian sent round a package, tied in glistening bow, containing a tantalizingly diaphanous bra and panties set. Unable to appreciate Aunt Vivian's nudge toward stylish hanky-panky, I tore through the remainder of tissue paper, still hoping to find there a buried check, money desperation overshadowing all other considerations. During the rifling, your grandmother entered the room and cast an eye on the box in my lap. Her mouth (and only her mouth) said: "How pretty." "Yes," I agreed. "Hand wash only," your grandmother said, and I seconded. "You'll need to be extra careful with those," your grandmother said, the "careful" applicable to much else besides easily shredded undies. Whatever else might be said about mother/daughter shorthand, it's a communication marvel. Understated but efficient, elliptical but exact, yes?

Love,
Aunt K

DeeDee,

Although the darkest of birth control's Dark Ages had passed by the time I turned twenty, there were infirmary physicians who objected to dispensing contraceptives and made sure no undergrad female left the examining table without being chided for engaging in—or planning to engage in—"cavalier intercourse." In the infirmary lottery, my roommate and I drew the same anti-libertarian medical practitioner. Both of us wanted IUDs. Voicing a preference: big mistake. The decision left to him, I'd get nothing, the doctor informed me, repeating that comment, word for word, to my roommate. As Diane di Prima complained: "The pill…makes you fat…it makes you hungry It gives you sore breasts." Also cysts in the case of my roommate and in my case severe leg cramps. Norinyl 1/80: powerful stuff. The pill's side effects aside, no one in my gal group preferred iffy condoms, the preventive upon which your grandparents courageously relied. One afternoon while shucking corn on the porch, your grandmother confided that your granddad, coming from a family of nine children, would have liked more children. She, coming from a family of thirteen children, wanted only your dad and me. "Two we could afford," she said. Unable to fast alight on a suitable response to that confidence, I responded not at all.

Love,
Aunt K

DeeDee,

Your au courant mother (and her grounded good sense) spared you any number of misapprehensions surrounding what your grandmother referred to as "the monthly flow." In your case: menstruation was discussed (before the event) with neither sighs nor lamentations, proving (yet again) that frank discussion versus terse allusion benefits most of us, including your thirteen-year-old self. Four years short of thirteen, I breezily returned from school to find your grandmother examining with consternation my previous day's underwear. The "bleeding" had started and vigorously continued in increasingly copious amounts for 10 days straight, the first installment of a trend that eventually lead to pelvic exams and hormone shots on a biweekly basis to regulate my rambunctious "flow." The stereotype of country girls "developing early" notwithstanding, I was the only one of my friends who had to lug around sanitary pads in her book bag. Not fun. Ever so fondly do I remember the teacher (a woman, mind you!) who pulled me aside, fifth grade, to rebuke me for piling books in my lap (the counter pressure helped with cramps) because "the boys are wondering why." The boys are wondering why. Are you bark-laughing, niece? Are you?

Love,
Aunt K

DeeDee,

Apparently your aunt has reached a stage in life when beaus of yesteryear "get back in touch," seized with the urge to "meet for a drink" or "grab a cup of coffee." The first fellow, prior to our re-meet, sent a meager spray of carnations with a "so looking forward" card tucked among the brown-edged blooms. Him I met for dinner at a god-awful Bavarian restaurant (his choice) and at the sight of me he exclaimed: "Damn it! You haven't changed!" Was this his idea of charming? My brow furrowed—a swift start to a long ordeal. The next guy, over coffee, wanted to enlist my help in recasting our dating debacle as the best of times. I'd have none of it. He'd been a prick, was a prick, and— no skin in the game—I called him one. Infuriatingly he smiled and judged me "still feisty." The third reconnector, I, with some difficulty, forced to pick up the bar tab because 1) I'd driven farthest and 2) he admitted he'd just "wanted to see which of us had more hair." He still had plenty. Such entertainment should come with a price tag. But how I do go on when the nub of this rant is basic beware: don't count on having seen the last of past lovers. Some roll back in with the tide.

Love,
Aunt K

DeeDee,

Regaling a reporter about Oxford, Mississippi, wooing customs, recently widowed Estelle Faulkner described a friend as having been "courted to death" by an admirer. Your grandmother and great-aunts used the very same expression. Eavesdropping, why hadn't my always alarmable self become alarmed by the description? I can only conclude that any burgeoning horror on my part was nipped in the bud by my elders' cheerful delivery of that word salad. I'm also reasonably certain that they, along with Mrs. Faulkner, were referencing a suitor's commendable persistence versus the terrorizing tactics of a stalker. Still: the phrase itself. Too similar to "hounded to death" for your aunt's liking or comfort. The Estelle Faulkner link isn't helping, either. To postpone indefinitely her first-round nuptials, Estelle took various evasive actions, none ultimately successful. And then, once successfully divorced, came her no-picnic union with Bill.

Love,
Aunt K

DeeDee,

Seldom (openly) referred to within the family: my six weeks as a student at the Tara Lara School of Dog Grooming. In residence, I gained a tremendous amount of weight and won a trophy for most dogs groomed, a statuette that thereafter languished in your grandparents' attic (yet another reminder of yet another life detour). Pointers learned: chalk fingers before attempting to pluck the ear hairs of any dog and never put your hand into a grooming cage that contains a Chow without the owner at your side. While in Albuquerque, I escaped dog bite but on second acquaintance with the city's airport ripped a hole in my skirt, the skirt's expandable waistband having caught on the door handle of the restroom stall as I exited. (If looking for omens, omens will be found.) To read on my eastbound flight, I carried Didion's *A Book of Common Prayer*. Charlotte Douglas's drift, Grace Strasser-Mendana's dying. An amazingly apt as well as unfortunate choice of narratives for a passenger who didn't want to arrive where she'd be arriving or encounter the person who'd there be waiting. Almost a decade passed before I ventured west again. An inducement for *you* to come quicker: no notes in your mailbox for the duration.

Love,
Aunt K

DeeDee,

No, I've not forgotten the one month, nine days, and three-quarter hour you refused to communicate with me because I'd stuck my nose where it didn't belong and judged your then-boyfriend Todd to be less than witty. Since you've since moved on, I'll snatch the liberty of expressing myself more bluntly here. The guy had the wit of a gnat, if that. Your parents agreed but had the sense to allow you to detect Todd's deficiencies at your own pace. As much as I'd like to pinky swear to stay forever out of your love life, should you decide to, say, wing it to Vegas, final destination Little White Wedding Chapel, Todd-ite in tow, I'd economy fly in quick pursuit, resolved to hunt you down on whatever strip of paved desert you trod and body-block your person from any state of Nevada official licensed to bless an ill-conceived union. Marriages are not as simple to get out of as your parents' example might have you believe.

Love,
Aunt K

DeeDee,

Tooling around the Parthenon during the shank of a very warm afternoon, consulting guidebook descriptions of virgins and cults and temples, my groom-to-be and I circled a stone column and very nearly smacked into his departmental colleague and colleague's wife, after which the four of us convened for a dinner that in substance if not menu could have taken place in the college town I thought we'd left behind. My reaction? Hyperventilating claustrophobia. As if a Greek god/goddess had sucked every particle of oxygen from the atmosphere. As if on that stony hill I'd plunged straight into the catacombs. As if the surreal notion that no one could go anywhere without being found had been decisively confirmed. I was outwardly so young on that pile of ancient rocks and inwardly so…something else. Worse: I did not love the one I was with. Questionable content, I realize, to pass along to a never-wed such as yourself. But of all the lies and fibs and half-truths that shore up your aunt's existence, I did, at the start of this correspondence, vow to tell you none. Much went missing in your aunt's marriage. Missing most prominently in her divorce: baseline civility.

Love,
Aunt K

DeeDee,

Further reason for your aunt to feel indebted to your great-aunt Vivian: Aunt Vivian's stalwart support after I slunk back home, an almost unmarried woman. When I summoned the nerve to appear in her public domain (the P.O.), she ditched workplace etiquette, sped around the counter, gave me a bracing hug and declared: "We're behind you." Whereupon I burst into tears. I was an emotional cyclone; Aunt Vivian had never before hugged me and I was tremendously, soggily, grateful for the break in precedent. I also blubbered because, despite Aunt Vivian's assurances, I had the *distinct* impression that not *all* our mutual relatives "had my back." I *strongly* suspected (in circulation) a certain minority report that judged me a foolish, impulsive girl, unable to make up her fickle mind. Fickle and flighty—neither a prized attribute within the family. Added to those weeping prods: the embarrassing, upsetting awareness that the generosity Aunt Vivian showed me had not been shown her. As all knew, Aunt Vivian had herself made a miserable marriage but stuck with the bad bargain. No one in the family would have proclaimed "we're behind you" to a bolter of Aunt Vivian's generation or encouraged defection of any stripe. Until your dad and I ruined the family's perfect record, no one had filed for divorce. Marriages, however miserable, carried forth.

Love,
Aunt K

DeeDee,

I revealed Aunt Vivian's support out of sequence. Before I could stake out the post office for my divorce docs, I had to relocate. Allotted an hour to clear self and stuff from the house my spouse retained, I coordinated with your father, who arrived on the dot, utility trailer in tow. In a pinch, your dad and I form a magnificently efficient twosome, which on this morning meant maximal hefting, minimal conversation. Maneuvering your great-grandmother's blanket chest down two sets of narrow stairs took some doing, but despite scraped elbows and shins we kept at it until my life possessions (or the percentage I'd been granted) got wedged in, tied down, and made road worthy. On the other end your grandfather assisted, balancing on an extension ladder as the three of us worked to drag and heave my stash through the window of the attic, there to nest on makeshift planks for the foreseeable future. For one terrifying moment, your granddad, bearing the full weight of the blanket chest upon him, wobbled on the ladder rungs, veins swelling, neck flushed. It's that image, that danger, I recall, recalling how much I imposed on the family during my drawn-out period of addled confusion. Thanks to them I was safe. I was also (thanks to me) a colossal screw-up.

Love,
Aunt K

DeeDee,

If I didn't say previously, I quite liked the house your dad helped me to (partially) pack up and forever depart at the end of my short-run marriage. Tin roof, floor-to-rafter bookshelves, indestructible brick floors. Cherished centerpiece: a resurrected farm table, perfect but for a tiny strip of wood gone missing at its center (no symbolism backtalk, please). Regardless of the quandary of how we'd have gotten that beauty through your grandparents' attic window, I'd have fought to keep possession if your dad's utility trailer could have transported it. Where that farm table stood and where I left it: three paces from a row of south-facing windows, six rush-seat chairs at its edges, four of those seats rarely occupied but on call should a full-house occasion arise. Also left behind: scads of houseplants—aloe, jade, weeping fig—my skip-out their death warrant. The theory that one incessantly recreates the same living space for oneself, regardless of locale? Well, maybe. If that person is the person in charge of finances. In subsequent temporary lodgings, I and my glassfuls of Queen Anne's lace and other flowering weeds got made wicked fun of. But by then I'd learned my lesson re: houseplant accumulation. Why collect what I'd have to discard?

Love,
Aunt K

DeeDee,

Your grandparents and I first met your mother when she and your dad drove in for the weekend—a visit that couldn't have been without anxiety for your dad, concerned as he must have been about receptions. (Not in terms of what we'd think of your mother; rather, what your mother might make of us.) The day was dreary and damp and so our living room looked more dreary and damp than usual. Adding to the dampness, I'd miscalculated their arrival time and was just out of the shower—a crushing turn of events. I'd desperately wanted to make a good impression on your mother and how could that be accomplished with a "wet head"? They sat close together, your parents, on the couch, your mother with her standout elegance looking like someone from another world (as she was). And yet she behaved as nervously as your father, holding his hand, working hard to make us like *her*, as if any other outcome were possible. It was obvious she adored your dad, and anyone who adored your dad had the inside track to our affections. But the truth is, quite apart from her adoration of our son and brother, we fell madly in love with your mother that afternoon. Every last one of us.

Aunt K

DeeDee,

Among the items resettled in your grandparents' attic after my marriage tanked: my wedding dress. I didn't haul it home because I was fond of the garment—the dress wasn't anything special, not even a wedding dress, per se. I threw it into your dad's utility trailer during the move-out because I didn't want to provide the contents for a ritualistic bonfire in my absence. Therein the irony. After the dress turned yellow in your grandparents' attic, I burned it myself in the backyard oil drum. "The dead whiteness of the dress made me more of a corpse than a bride but I hadn't enough energy to infuriate my mother by telling her so." Spot on, but I couldn't quote Alice Thomas Ellis in my twenties because I hadn't read her novels yet and your grandmother was more dismayed than infuriated by the whole wedding business, so the second clause wouldn't have applied. Your mother's own wedding dress drama—you've heard about it, I suppose? In the run-up to the big day, your other grandmother decided your mother's satin mini was two inches too mini and returned it for additional hemline alterations. Your mother only discovered the tampering while dressing for the ceremony. There were tears; there were threats of refusing to come downstairs in it, the new proportions all wrong. None of this we knew, waiting below.

Love,
Aunt K

DeeDee,

What wedding dress ruminations churned up last night, late night: the memory of your granddad in a womanless wedding, playing bridesmaid to the Ruritan Club president's bride. The show's portly star wore a blonde wig and a whipped-up-for-the-occasion frock with burst seams (part of the joke, as your grandmother had to explain). Most of your granddad's costume was improvised from family holdings. He made his womanly debut wearing one of his sister's "let out" dresses, satiny green with black trim, a black wig and generous smears of rouge and lipstick. I can't remember your dad's reaction, but I was *transfixed*—as was every other five-year-old sitting with Mom in the audience watching Dad play a woman who wasn't. According to the historians, womanless weddings have been around since the nineteenth century and struck up in the South—a transfixing tidbit in and of itself. Because how often does nineteenth-century South and transgressive hijinks appear in the same paragraph? In Mrs. James W. Hunt's 1918 *Womanless Wedding* script, producers were urged to cast "prominent men" and insist they "wear ladies' shoes." The burning question: which pair of ladies' clodhoppers did your granddad cram his size eleven, double D-width trotters into? Sorry to say I haven't a clue.

Love,
Aunt K

DeeDee,

Your mother's desire for an at-home wedding also (I gather) involved a tense test of wills. The sticking point: your other grandmother considered their Greensboro house too small a venue. Even filled with guests, waiters, a musical trio, instruments, and urns sprouting magnolia and holly, it seemed roomy to us. Beyond the patio, a few hardy golfers played through on the green, despite the squally December weather. Your mother's father didn't attend because he thought your mother, at twenty-one, too young to marry, and because he'd vowed never to return to property he'd forfeited in the divorce settlement. Therefore it was your mother's mother who walked her down the stairs, neither betraying a whiff of upset or discord from their earlier contretemps. After the I do's, the photographer arranged our original family of four in a semi-circle and started clicking. Your father holds an empty champagne glass, his new gold wedding band gleaming. Your grandfather seems to be holding his breath. Your grandmother's orchid corsage rides high on her shoulder. I appear off balance, one foot too close to the other. No one is full out grinning, not because it wasn't a happy occasion but because at least three of us didn't want to come off as riotous country bumpkins, inadvertently embarrassing your dad. Before she and your dad made their getaway, your mother hugged us, her new in-laws. Before driving off ourselves, we made sure to extend appreciative goodbyes to your other grandmother. During that exchange, no one, either side, stepped in for the hug.

Love,
Aunt K

West Coast
Wednesday, Sept. 25

DeeDee,

Your dad stayed long enough in Vegas for the rubber supporting the side mirrors of his Nissan truck to disintegrate in the heat. I stayed long enough to eat porterhouse steak at three a.m. and wonder at the connections between marriages and parched earth. I don't know this personally, but I've been told that one must arrive in Vegas armed with the dates of previous divorce decrees as well as the current addresses of exes in order to obtain the next marriage license—necessities that must dampen any enthusiasm to "try again." Although the date of my divorce decree is burned into my brain, subjected to the rack I wouldn't be able to provide the locational specifics of my former spouse. (Having devoted *strenuous* effort to forgetting all that could be forgotten, why would I jeopardize marital amnesia by keeping tabs on my ex and his neighborhood?) In my experience, a ridiculous number of people assume a busted marriage represents a standing invitation to offer up extensive, unsolicited feedback. One such pass-along: my matrimonial gamble categorized as a "mistake" I'd "never repeat." Even in the grips of full-blown escape mania, I found the appraisal peculiar. Was the assumption that, post-mistake, I'd turned into a totally different person, none of my previous wants and wishes sticking around to motivate future behaviors? What an extraordinary notion.

Love,
Aunt K

DeeDee,

Your paternal grandparents married in secret. Shocking, isn't it? Because they continued to live apart as singles, to counteract intimations of "loose morals" should your grandmother find herself pregnant, each told a sister. (Your grandmother didn't get pregnant—not while the marriage remained secret.) The trouble with secrets: not everyone is equally skilled at keeping them. Your grandmother told her sister Clara (who did keep her mouth shut). The sister your grandfather told (who shall remain nameless) instantly told your great-grandmother, who told your great-grandfather, who told who knows how many because your great-grandfather considered secret marriages ridiculous. Your grandmother's high school scrapbooks preserve one—and only one—*extremely* brief letter from your grandfather during their courting days. In it, your grandfather confirms plans to meet up after the ballgame, later in the week. "I will tell you everything Wed. night," he writes. When that missive ended up in my grabby hands, I quizzed writer and recipient separately as to what that "everything" entailed. Neither could remember—or much cared by then. Only their daughter cared, "everything" such a huge and captivating promise.

Love,
Aunt K

DeeDee,

You've noticed, I'm sure, that while I've gone on and on about the end of my own marriage, I've said little about your parents'. Avoidance, pure and simple. This month (previously, too) I've been circling the subject of their split because, despite the time gap between then and now, I'd rather not admit (or believe) it happened. Your parents' divorce was infinitely more distressing than mine—on your dad (of course), but also on your grandparents and (yes) on me. Because we believed in your parents' coupledom, you see. Believed in its rightness, its fitness, its resiliency. Proved wrong, we not only lost the regular companionship of your mother, we lost faith in the accuracy of our perceptions, in our interpretation of the manifestly true. In terms of age and wedding dates, your dad and I divorced out of sequence. I was twenty-six when I called it quits, a mere year and a half into the contract. Your parents' union lasted twelve times that. I so vividly remember opening your dad's letter on the icy steps of the Northampton post office. My nose was running from the cold; I'd forgotten to bring gloves. Because I read at a standstill, people complained; I was blocking their path. But still I didn't move. I assume your father wrote not trusting himself (or me) to discuss it over the phone. He gave no reason for the separation in the letter. Neither he nor your mother ever shared the reason/reasons. For me to speculate here would be heretical, disrespectful of that discretion. But I do brood about their breakup. To this hour, I brood and miss your mother terribly.

Love,
Aunt K

OCTOBER NOTES

[Destroyed]

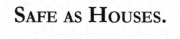

SAFE AS HOUSES.

DeeDee,

As a child, which event exposed you to the terrible truth that not everything could be made better, the surrounding adults as incapable as yourself? For me and my friends it was a classmate's accidental shooting of her older sister. None of the community's comfort rituals seemed remotely up to the task of lessening the family's grief: visits to the house, paying respects in the very room where the dead had suddenly, violently died, bringing casseroles and cakes to three survivors who couldn't bear to eat. No one blamed Debbie—she and Diana were just kids, playing. And no one blamed Mr. Baker, however much he blamed himself. Keeping loaded guns in the house was a community practice and remained so. A week after the funeral, Debbie returned to school, our new, intense, ultra-friendly attentions further upending her world. Rehearsing for the spring cantata at the time, I sang my Queen-of-the-Fairies lines waving around a magic wand your grandmother had constructed from scrap wood and aluminum foil. It wasn't as if I'd believed in magic or magic wands prior to the accident, but afterwards playacting those beliefs seemed a... *travesty*, I would have said, if I'd known the word. Our yearbook that year carried a full-page memorial to Diana. I have my copy still. Is it callous or kind to hope that between then and now Debbie mislaid hers?

Love,
Aunt K

DeeDee,

Did your parents share they'd considered building a house on a back acre of the farm? Their choice would have made a spectacular lot. Surrounded on three sides by old-growth oak and pine, they would have looked out onto open fields: a wide view from a protected spot. They would have lived Appleton's prospect-refuge theory of geographical contentment to a T. Since the woods hadn't then been cut for timber, you'd have had a choice of massive trees to climb or field rows to run. In any direction—north, south, east, or west—you wouldn't have felt penned in, not in the slightest. I understood your dad's wish to return home and work with your grandfather and because the idea meant so much to him felt grateful to your mom for supporting the plan. Your grandparents would have gladly given over the acreage, thrilled to have your parents live so close by. But the farm couldn't support two salaries then, perhaps never could. It was hard for your grandparents—hard to acknowledge their helplessness in the face of incontrovertible fact, extremely hard to disappoint your dad's hopes. I know it was hard because whenever your grandmother talked about that conversation, even after your grandfather died, she cried.

Love,
Aunt K

DeeDee,

A common sight in kudzu country: houses falling in on themselves, choked by vines, reclaimed by nature. "Left to rot," as your grandparents described the breach—not with admiration. But for me and my bicycle gang those dilapidated outposts were terrific fun. Abandoned houses = open houses. A two-pronged adventure, really: wheeling through an obstacle course of weeds and yard stumps to carouse interiors that barely were, holes in the walls and floorboards, swinging banisters, splintered steps. My best booty find was a pottery jug, missing just a chink of its lip, but I left it where it leaned because to cart home another old something? Why? Amazing that none of us broke legs or arms or punctured ourselves. More amazing: none of us wigged out over the ghost menace or thought twice about disturbing the maybe-not-entirely-departed with our marauding. Given the suggestibility of children, alert to every wrong wind and seeded silence, that aspect seems most puzzling to me now. But maybe any kid's universe is too full of the excitingly new to accommodate much else. Or am I misremembering?

Love,
Aunt K

DeeDee,

By talking tumble-downs I've probably given credence to the notion that your dad and I grew up in some kind of farming refugee camp. To set the record straight(er): three houses in the vicinity were listed on the National Register of Historical Places. Compared to the Thirties clapboard and Sixties brick that sprung up around them, those three classified as the community's grandees, though no native viewed them with anything approaching reverence. They were houses. People lived in them. End of discussion. The 19th-century building that got the most press, "Twin Houses," memorialized an estate squabble. Two inheritors fought to get (and show they'd gotten) precisely half of an inheritance. You've seen the house: two two-storey structures, built one in front of the other, connected in the middle, left side of Highway 34, just before the East Ridge turn-off. In grammar school, when I had to write a report on the house, your grandmother dutifully drove me over to chat with the local historian who lived there. A grandfather's clock ticked. Floorboards creaked. The air inside smelled of...not much. It was a house that had survived wars and the Southern clime but lacked spirit. One didn't come away with a sense that euphoric joy had lodged there in any century. Whatever the historian said, I wrote down, failing to ask a single follow-up question about any past resident, including the intriguingly named Affiah and Lovey. I could blame the house and its oppressiveness for that procedural snafu, but the fault was all mine. I was young, fast bored with history.

Love,
Aunt K

DeeDee,

Did you find overnighting at a pal's house disorienting when you were young? And why can't I remember whether you did or didn't? (We must have discussed sleepovers, good points and bad, at one time or another? While I babysat? At a family barbecue?) Given where and among whom your dad and I incubated, one might assume the insides of our friends' houses looked pretty much the same. Actually they varied quite a bit. Lyle F.'s kitchen had exposed rafters. "Florida Room" furniture overfilled Mary G.'s den. Susan B.'s house lacked knickknacks of any sort—not a single nonessential item on display anywhere. On the premises, in a house not your own, you'd have to watch how much you ate at supper and how you ate it. And whether or not your pal's house smelled wonderful, it smelled *different*. In a strange bed, even if you'd worn yourself out giggling and singing Leslie Gore choruses, there'd always be something a little off—scratchier sheets or flatter pillow or denser blanket—some divergence that interfered with thoughtless snooze. And if you got up to pee in the middle of the night, there'd be that moment of confusion: where were you and how did you get there? And then, come morning, you'd have to get dressed for breakfast because it wasn't *your* family you'd be sitting across from. I did like packing an overnight suitcase, though. What to leave in, what to leave out.

Love,
Aunt K

DeeDee,

When your great-grandfather and grandfather built your grandparents' house, they cut each board with a handsaw. As a teenager, to prove I could, I sawed one board in half and caught the teeth with every stroke. "Put more arm into it," I was told. The amount of "arm" that went into the house your dad and I grew up in beggars the imagination. And yet it was built. The bathroom/bedrooms extension, completed by your grandfather and a sidekick twenty years later, had the power tool advantage but not much luck, weather-wise. The scaffolding had just gone up when a freak snowstorm dumped five inches. Nothing else to take his time, your grandfather helped me build two snowmen in the yard but glanced repeatedly beyond our project to the stalled, his mind clearly on snow melt. Once the extension was finished, I had a new bedroom that looked out onto the backyard, a curve of woods, a wedge of field—none of it threatening in daylight. A different vista, though, backyard night.

Love,
Aunt K

DeeDee,

Painful memory: I'm in a stranger's arms, being carted down outside steps, *my* arms frantically reaching for the left-behind, mouth wailing. The rest is fuzzy. According to your grandmother, this seminal (for me) incident occurred at a cottage "past the pier" in Nags Head. A visiting teenager had asked permission to take me to the beach and your grandmother, no doubt delighted by the prospect of a childcare break, agreed to the handoff. Also, according to your grandmother: my short-term custodian was "a girl who loved babies, who just wanted to spend some time with you, play with you. You'd have thought you were being kidnapped." (And how was I to know I wasn't?) Because I put up such a howling fuss, the expedition was abandoned, the mom-in-training disappointed, your grandmother at pains to explain my non-embracing personality. In March of 1962 that same cottage, one of two separated by less than five feet of air and sand, got taken to sea by the Ash Wednesday storm. As a family we journeyed down to survey the wreckage, marveling yet again on the whys and hows of ocean snatching one structure while sparing the next. In one of my more maudlin phases at the time, I fixated on the mate-less-ness of the survivor cottage: how alone it seemed, how stranded. Since family maudlin phases come and go, shall we call them tidal?

Love from the hurricane-less coast,
Aunt K

West Coast
Friday, Nov. 8

DeeDee,

The Loma Prieta temblor. A seismic event that absorbed your attention or no? Although I wasn't around for the quake itself, I arrived in time for the aftershocks. Unsettling: the swaying of electrical wires in a windless moment. Although I've yet to dream of earthquakes, I suspect that night terror is in the works. You'll have no interest in your aunt's dreams (why should you?) but bear with me. There's a reason I bring up last night's night script. Instead of the usual scenario (tidal wave approaches while I stand paralyzed in its path), last night I was ahead of the game. A tidal wave still played a major part in the dramatics, but from a different angle. Through frantic (and dream-lengthy) effort, I managed to kick my way to the very crest of the water wall. The reward of that strenuous survival? A backside view of a multi-storey drop. If I had/were a therapist, I'd give the interpretation this spin: aging. You think you're in control, on "top of things" but the other-side plunge will be swift, frightening and ultimately fatal. Yes, I realize: getting-old yammerings are as boring as recycled dreams. But, you see, the actual point of my sharing is this: your aunt's not old. She's simply anticipating.

Love,
Aunt K

DeeDee,

Try though I might, I can't recall you warming to dollhouses or drawing on that structural assist to make-believe. My one and only dollhouse was the six-room Colonial model sold in the Montgomery Ward catalogue for four bucks. Just last week I happened upon its likeness in an antiques shop window, rust spots left untouched to prove authenticity. (Needless to say, last week's example cost more than four bucks.) My inherited version featured lithographed rugs and window box planters but little else. Most of the original furniture had been lost by the time it came into my keeping, so none of the six rooms were crammed with objects. Did that paucity of furnishings shape my notion of how much is too much in homescaping, incline me toward an anti-clutter esthetic? If so, exposure to your mother's mash-ups of art, books, tables, lamps, and overstuffed chairs squelched that early bias. Snuggled onto one or another cushion, you appeared (sorry if this offends) part of your mother's coherent design, as perhaps you were and are. And where's the harm in that?

Love,
Aunt K

West Coast
Sunday, Nov. 10

DeeDee,

Since you frequently switched bedrooms (and houses) as a child and appeared to take those transitions in stride, odds are my previous frightened-come-night note rang no bells. To be very clear, in daylight I was *thrilled* with my new bedroom and its expanded contents: double bed, side table, rocking chair, record player, three-drawer dresser, closet, and (in time) a snazzy powder-blue princess phone. I was a slob when it came to hanging up clothes but shoving furniture around? Favorite pastime. In homage, I wrote up a rearrangement saga—one-quarter actual, three-quarters fantasy—for the 4-H "Home Improvement" competition. Your grandmother, in the audience for my blue ribbon, managed to keep a poker face, listening to the Home Demonstration agent cum contest judge read off all that I'd improved, that public airing the first your grandmother had heard (or seen) of such. You'd (maybe?) be prouder of an aunt who copped to the invention and refused the plaudits. But what can I tell you? I was far too proud of my imaginary refurb to disown it—and even less willing to give up the medallion prize.

Love,
Aunt K

DeeDee,

Egged on by the same Home Demonstration agent who'd rewarded my fake home improvements, your grandmother returned from a Women's Club meeting primed to repaint the living room. Far from alone in her zeal, her sister clubwomen also went home determined to cover pale walls with the "latest color trend," a maroon-ish brown. At our house, once your grandmother had put away her paintbrush, a fairly small room appeared even smaller. Also light-parched. Day or evening, to see much of anything in it, every lamp had to be switched on. For a month or so, your grandfather—who until that remodeling project had voiced no opinion on home décor—read his newspaper surrounded by walls the color of a bruised peach. Then he requested a return to what had been. Your grandmother nodded—in total agreement. I (obnoxiously) clapped. As can be imagined, turning brown/maroon to white required more than a single coat. After that flurry of do and redo, our living room didn't see a lick of paint for years. I don't like to think therein the lesson: attempt different, live to regret. So I won't.

Love,
Aunt K

DeeDee,

Supposedly Georges Simenon called thirty-three houses home during his life span—which seems excessive until compared with his other numbers: 200-plus novels in his own name, another 200 written under seventeen pseudonyms. Where to go to tip one's hat in the case of Simenon? Which house of the thirty-three? The National Trust solved that dilemma for Woolf fans by taking over Monk's House. For the price of an entry ticket, any devotee can loom over Virginia's single bed and pillow, imagining that busy, busy brain of hers struggling to call it a night. Since Virginia herself made expeditions to the Brontës' parsonage, Shelley's rental in Lerici and Madame de Sevigné's chateau in Brittany, she must have anticipated, if not altogether welcomed, the swarm to come. Harder to countenance (given her income source): the repugnance of the caretaker who mocked, in print, two pilgrims she'd observed weeping at the author's presumed exit gate en route to the River Ouse. (The gate no longer exists.) I wept at no gates but found touring the green rooms Virginia's own sis mocked for their "ubiquitous" color a profoundly moving experience. A genius had lived and worked in those spaces. How could one not be affected? "I envy houses alone in the fields," Woolf wrote mere weeks before she took her life. Does my middlingly busy brain retain that line because of its sentiment, date penned (your grandmother's birthday), or the two in concert?

Love,
Aunt K

DeeDee,

Your dad and I made a terrible mistake the Christmas after your granddad died. We took your grandmother on a trip to Colonial Williamsburg, convinced that being away from home that first holiday would be less painful for her than the alternative. You remember the Williamsburg layout from school trips—the silversmith stall, the bindery, the tavern with upstairs lodging, twelve beds to a room. The streets and buildings, inside and out, were decorated to the max, festive for the holidays and tidy, so very tidy—history evoked without mud or stench. Your grandmother went along with "whatever we wanted to do" but her heart wasn't in it. She'd celebrated Christmas in her own house for forty-odd years; to be elsewhere only added to her sense of loss. When your dad and I realized our error, we should have packed up and headed south immediately. Instead we stayed, touring the attractions, listening to professional carolers, eating turkey in a hotel restaurant where your dad and I drank too much without parental reprimand for the first and only time in our lives, all of us out of place, grieving. Back on home turf, hauling her suitcase from the car trunk, your grandmother announced in no uncertain terms: "I want to spend next Christmas here." However empty the house seemed without your granddad, it was her empty house.

Love,
Aunt K

DeeDee,

Awake too late, awake without wanting to be, I try to defeat insomnia by taking a mental tool-around your grandparents' house. It's not a conscious decision—or not entirely conscious. If you're wondering why someone who left home so long ago persists in circling back to reset her sleep clock, you're not alone. Nevertheless: to your grandparents' house I go. If touring the perimeters doesn't put me out, I move on to room-by-room surveys—a brass bowl here, a desk calendar there, the soap dish beside the sink where your grandmother washed my hair until I was six, rolled towel under my forehead for padding. If I'm still wide-eyed after those circuits, my cataloging rises to the attic's old, older, oldest storage—stuff your dad and I will eventually have to inventory for real, deciding what to keep, what to let go. Those are the bad nights, when my house review extends as far and as high as the attic. Will your dad and I manage to save the house where we slept as babies? And if we can't, how to bear the parting?

Love,
Aunt K

CALIFORNIA.

DeeDee,

The house I live in now (a superfluous description if you'd visit) is a 764-square-foot brown-shingled cottage one street off the main drag. Acquiring it required a background check, two months rent and security deposit up front. If not awake at five and first to call the listing (at 6:45 a.m.), I'd have lost the privilege of gutting my bank account for purposes of shelter. By nine, as my landlord still glories in reminding, fifty-eight hopefuls waited for my check to bounce or rap sheet to surface. Although I wouldn't wish insomnia on a snake, credit where credit's due: it's a fetching cottage, if a bit tatty. (Why upgrade in the face of fifty-plus rental applicants?) Cracked windowpanes, a gouge in the shower stall, dry rot threading the threshold, canted kitchen floor. However: whoever lives in this zip code lives mainly outside, and the yard is a showstopper: pink and white trellis roses, lilac, rosemary, a bountiful loquat tree, and ivy leaves big as baseballs. I'm told this rental came through the Loma Prieta quake with flying colors, but other bungalows in town weren't so fortunate. On after-supper strolls, I pass red-tagged structures by the score. They look like hurricane wreckage, those skewed foundations and caved in-walls. Except I no longer live in the land of hurricanes; I live where earth waves. (Still) something of an adjustment.

Love,
Aunt K

DeeDee,

You've been in my Honda hatchback: very limited space. On the drive out, I had to restrict my cargo to the flat-ish, foldable, and compact. Heirlooms that made the cut: a throw your grandmother assembled from clothing scraps; your great-grandfather's (miniature) toolbox; the blue pitcher your great-grandmother used to water flowers and I to display them. It was only somewhere in Texas that I realized I'd packed nothing of your grandfather's, an oversight that bothered me at the time and haunted me after his death, that lack of something of his travelling with me too emblematic, too predictive. When I disappeared into the shed after the funeral, I was searching for the paddle he and I used to maneuver around stumps in Indiantown creek. At the UPS office in E. City, the clerk calculated the price of shipping it to California (ridiculously high due to the paddle's dimensions), then paused operations to "double-check." In light of the expense, was I "still sure" I wanted to send it? Rarely have I spoken as rudely as I did answering that question. But what did I expect? It wasn't her father's paddle. What she saw was splintered wood, not grief.

Love,
Aunt K

West Coast
Wednesday, Dec. 4

DeeDee,

The two-mile jam up during today's commute was caused by a chest of drawers that had tipped off somebody's ride and landed on its side, middle lane. Edging past at walking speed, we, the delayed, had more than enough time to eyeball the obstruction and pity/curse whoever had gone light on the bungee cords. During his open-truck moving era, your dad secured (some might say over-secured) his tie-downs with a combination of Boy Scout knots. Nothing ever fell off but, destination reached, untying time had to be factored in. Your dad helped move me twice in-state; your grandparents, twice in-state and once from Massachusetts, a more complicated transfer because of the distance and an unhappy cat. In my last college move, your granddad and I got caught in a vicious rain and windstorm outside Roanoke Rapids that ripped the plastic off the painted boards and cinderblocks that constituted my bookshelves. Loading up similar shelving in Massachusetts, he said: "Daughter, this is the last time I'm moving cinderblocks." I saw his point but stuck to my preferences. Every piece of my California furnishings can fast be disassembled for reassembly elsewhere. Even so, next move, I'm going to have to pare down my book cache, the overflow now forming a row of leaning towers. But what to relinquish? And what if I change my mind? And what if I can't replace what I've tossed? I'm not as skilled as either of your parents at recognizing when to let go and following through on the intuition. Fortunately you live closer to their examples. The family harbors enough of my kind.

Love,
Aunt K

West Coast
Thursday, Dec. 5

DeeDee,

This note in praise of the fabulous Dot, who lives within view of the Hollywood sign and has an outdoor deck built around a stupendous live oak. Hands down, the most charming individual I've met since arrival and, for whoever takes the time to listen, a raconteur of the first order. Brief summary here. An Eastern lass, Dot came west from New York in the Forties, signed on as a secretary at one of the studios and had a front row seat for various studio shenanigans as well as Rock Hudson's first screen test. ("No one was bowled over by his acting, but he looked smashing.") As part of her working gal wardrobe, Dot wore choker pearls, a "secretarial standard" of the time. Despite her "marginally diverting" job, Dot soon recognized she was "too much of a book girl" to work "in the industry" long-term. Of the suitors swirling round, she chose a professor. Her living room has a peaked ceiling and redwood beams and built-in bookshelves on every wall. We sipped tea as the afternoon zipped along and the bon mots accumulated. (And your aunt with no tape recorder to properly record them!) As I very sorrowfully took my leave, Dot took my hand and invited me back for an overnight. "And I don't extend that invitation to just anybody," she clarified. I was enormously touched in the moment and later enormously perturbed by Dot's lack of audience. Why aren't more of us sitting down to tea, listening to the Dots?

Love,
Aunt K

DeeDee,

Should you be curious: no one ever inquires of a California transplant why she came. The operating assumption seems to be that anyone who can manage to get here will hasten to do so for one or more of the usual, unassailable motives. The climate. The gold. The re-start. Since I'd rather not try to explain what I haven't yet completely figured out, I appreciate the policy of non-interrogation. I've become less happy, a few seasons into the experiment, with the corollary assumption that because I'm here I ascribe to the doctrine that whatever needs improving will, here, inevitably improve/regenerate/reboot. Did your aunt once buy into the hype, convince herself she'd get another chance to carve out an alternate destiny if she made the forty-five-hour, 2,976.2-mile drive, home to here? Yeah. She did. Realities since revealed: any transplant remains a surface cruiser and (duh) endless opportunities for the asking is a false pitch. In the Golden State, as elsewhere, one needs her claws.

Love,
Aunt K

West Coast
Thursday, Dec. 12

DeeDee,

Regardless of whether anyone *here* cares why I'm in CA, I'd prefer a credible alibi. One I've flirted with: after a Southerner tries north, where else to venture but west? Another: it makes a certain logical sense to exchange a past-soaked place for a future-obsessed place to test how the reorientation sits. Not bad, either cover story. Except: "You have to take yourself wherever you go."(Beryl Bainbridge) Except: "You try to live as if nothing had ever happened. But it's useless." (J.G. Farrell) What I've picked up in the California trenches, as opposed to California library stacks: plenty have stalled here while vigorously pretending otherwise. I understand the stall; I also commiserate with the denial. We're all clinging to the edge in more ways than three. But the failure to admit to failure is starting to feel more wearying than the weight of your aunt's accumulated past. It takes a lot of effort, niece: continuously charging forward, staring squarely ahead. How about this defense? I came to California because I needed to get out of my own story for a while and didn't think that could be accomplished staying where I started. Does that excuse pass muster? Sound more believable? Less? You pick.

Love,
Aunt K

West Coast
Tuesday, Dec. 17

DeeDee,

As it happens, I'm not the first in the extended family to take on a California address. Somewhere outside of San Diego, a second or third or fourth cousin resides. Moved out in the Fifties with her Navy-enlisted husband and stayed put. According to your grandmother, I met that California-based relative when she visited one summer to catch up with cartloads of kin. (What I most remember about the get-together: a different distant cousin walking around with a fishhook in her cheek, the result of her brother's bad cast.) Another of your grandmother's relatives tested out his new motorcycle by driving it cross-country, East Coast to West. He only stayed in California long enough to gas up, then wheeled around and headed back. (Your dad derives no end of hilarity from that story.) Although my neighbor's daughter doesn't seem to own a motorcycle, she prefers the Harley set. Guardians elsewhere, she hosts biker parties that spill onto the upper and lower decks of her parents' house and into the yard. Despite the overflow, neighborly courtesies have (thus far) been maintained. No raucous squalling, no plein air screwing (on my side of the hedge), empty beer cans flung at her parents' loquat (not mine).

Love,
Aunt K

DeeDee,

If I keep to my no-more-Woolf pledge, will you permit some rhapsodizing over Kenneth Millar, aka Ross Macdonald? In Santa Barbara, at various times, he lived on Cliff Drive, Bay Road, Via Esperanza, Chelham Way, Camino de la Luz and Bath Street. The Bath Street house (acquired for $7,000 in the Forties) currently overlooks a parking lot, a neighborhood downgrade that hasn't affected the property value as much as a non-Californian might suppose. Macdonald was into Freud. He and penultimate Southern gal Eudora Welty were devoted friends. The producer of "American Family" approached him for recommendations of real-life Santa Barbara families that matched his creations in *The Underground Man*. A "hard-boiled" crime novelist lauded for plot, but what about those ravishing descriptions? One example from zillions: returning to L.A., the ever-roaming Detective Lew Archer observes "an unbroken stream of headlights pour(ing) toward us, as if the city was leaking light through a hole in its side." Understood: you'll need to get a little longer in the tooth to fully appreciate the content of this next Macdonald sentence, but for the time being enjoy the music of its rollout: "I lapsed for a while into my freeway daydream: I was mobile and unencumbered, young enough to go where I had never been and clever enough to do new things when I got there…" Did Macdonald's California novels play a part in your aunt's migration patterns? I expect so. I expect so.

Love,
Aunt K

West Coast
Thursday, Dec. 19

DeeDee,

The light *is* different here—there's no arguing the point. When feeling discouraged in the Golden State, my Boston native officemate fishes out a photo of herself wearing a huge white puffer jacket among snowdrifts. (Her "polar bear ensemble," she calls it.) If that ploy fails to stiffen her resolve, she takes her next morning's coffee onto the balcony of her apartment to be seduced anew by California glow. Even in December, the light here is more amber than gray. My favorite part of late-afternoon meetings is the afterwards, when I get to stroll across a deserted campus and foot drag to my heart's content, charmed to distraction by the valediction of Bay Area day on mulberry and stone. The oldest of the university's surviving grads matriculated in view of sweeping orchards. At alumni events, when they huddle and reminisce, I'm all ears. When they say "hard to picture now," I nod, picturing away: low-hanging, luscious fruit, sure, but also the spectacle of row after row, acre upon acre of fruit trees saturated in California light. Depending on which source you trust, "earthquake light" is scientific fact or crackpot theory. (I'm rooting for crackpot.) Last week, at work, I participated in my fifth earthquake drill. A straightforward matter of duck and cover when someone's at her desk. But if she's caught outside, staring at the light? On that eventuality, I've not been prepped.

Love,
Aunt K

DeeDee,

I returned to the cottage yesterday to find my landlord had been busy in my absence, chopping down the ivy extension I'd cultivated as privacy screen between my back steps and my to-the-north neighbors' kitchen window. It took a while to fix on the culprit, and during that while I mentally ran through an alarmingly lengthy list of persons known to be holding active grudges against me, followed by a backup list of persons who *probably* wouldn't mind settling older scores should a choice opportunity arise. Then I realized those named on both lists worked nine to five, same as me, and no way/no how would any of them use up a sick day on foliage revenge. When I called the landlord, he said yes, he'd "stopped by," that "vines rot shingles," and he'd "taken care of the problem." So I ate my dinner cornflakes with a view of withering vines, which will soon drop away and, if I stay put at this address, once again expose my closest neighbors to me and me to them. Such is a renter's dilemma and a downside of what your grandmother refers to as my "flit about" lifestyle. Do I want to move (again)? I could do without this landlord, but I'd miss Leona, the neighborhood cat. Another California transplant proclivity: as fresh arrivals, we tend to exult. Talking to your granddad my first week in the Pacific standard time zone, I said: "I really like it here, Dad," and he said: "Well, good then. Good." It was our last conversation, your grandfather's and mine. And because it was, I sometimes think the true reason I stay west is to preserve that "good then, good," to remain where he thought I'd contentedly landed, where he thought he'd left me, where I was when we lost him.

Love,
Aunt K

DeeDee,

The Downtown Association has strung colored lights on the palm trees and rigged up a skating rink in the square and local celebrity Peggy Fleming has agreed to show up in skates as part of the evening's festivities. Since dusk, the entire length of Main Street has been given over to horse-drawn carriages and jaywalking shoppers on the hunt for last-minute candles and cashmere and travel packages to Baja. Every shop will stay open till midnight—a Chamber of Commerce guarantee. Until your parents split up, I spent Christmas Eve helping to wrap your loot once you'd conked out. As I date it, you gave up St. Nick at the respectable age of five. Your aunt procrastinated. Even after the actual mechanics appeared dubious (flying reindeer, etc.), I held to the notion of Santa Claus roaming our floorboards. It was the magic I hesitated to renounce. Because if you *believe* something magical has transpired in the living room at midnight, you still *feel* the remnants of that pizzazz, crack of dawn. The Christmas I asked for a toy mouse for the cat, Santa Claus (your grandmother writing with her left hand) Scotch-taped a note to the RCA Victor TV, explaining he was "all out of mice" but enjoyed the snack. It's extraordinary—or funny? or sad?—how speedily I can re-inhabit that state of tremulous bliss, clutching what I thought Santa had scrawled upon. Rousted from bed, your grandparents and groggy dad, good sports all, oohed and ahed over what they already knew lodged beneath the tree. Unlike other big brothers, your dad didn't ruin the day or the myth for me. He let me believe that a guy in a red suit popped into our farmhouse for as long as I needed to believe in guy, suit, and visit. Reason enough to feel grateful your dad is my bro—as if I needed another.

Love,
Aunt K

EPHEMERA.

Dear DeeDee,

I like to think that, had you existed, I'd have written to you precisely as I've written in these notes. I like to think that writing about semi-ancient family history to a figment of my imagination isn't solely the result of my brother and me being the last of our line, no one after us to tell our stories to, no one to remember those stories, no one who will pass those stories along. I like to think that the motivation fueling these notes to a nonexistent niece can't be chalked up to mere ego, mere sentiment, mere regret at not being anyone's aunt or mother or the sheer dread of being closer to silenced as a storyteller myself. But I am not quite that shameless a liar. Not yet.

Love,
Aunt K

Author's Note

In the words of critic Jacqueline Rose:
"Memory is defensive, recalcitrant."
Other than the nonexistent niece, all content is as true as
defensive, recalcitrant memory allows.

ACKNOWLEDGMENTS

Versions of some of these notes first appeared in *a) glimpse) of,* *Glint Literary Journal, Lunch, The Midnight Oil, Queen Mob's Tea House/Misfit Docs, Southern Women's Review* and *Wraparound South.*